Dying for Living

Sins & Confessions of a Hollywood Villain & Libertine Patriot

PATRICK KILPATRICK

BOULEVARD BOOKS
The New Face of Publishing
www.BoulevardBooks.org
ISBN 13 : 9781942500445

Dying for Living

Sins & Confessions of a Hollywood Villain & Libertine Patriot

Upbringing

Patrick Kilpatrick

The names of certain people (those not celebrities in the public eye) have been changed to preserve their identity and privacy.

The quotes and lines at the beginnings of each chapter come either from my gorged 'anaconda blood-root loosed from me trousers' on set improvisations while acting a character, or the skilled hands of scriptwriters involved – be they desperate neophyte film school graduates to zenith Elmore Leonard or stub cigar chomping bon vivant Spielberg – to name drop two rare creative rockets cascading over polluted and inspiring atmospheres with whom I've worked … or from scripts I have written. I adore fine writing. In its absence from a script one chooses literate improvisation or stripping from the gifted anywhere – always a famished orphaned boar rifling trash for a sweet fungal verbal morsel.

Un-indicted co-conspirators and colluders

In any endeavor of this type there are gang members, indispensable criminal confederates.

Jack Mulholland - his photo archival skill and pro devotion, Tori Whitney Lalond - early proofing when no one was there, Natasha Kertes - jacket photo artistry (vanity or posing never involved, she enters a space and seizes the essence of her subject), Christopher Hassett at RiotMaterial.com - cogent editing, Cassandra Campbell, Michael Levine, Eileen and Joey Lauren Koch - PR consultation at many junctures, Greg Forest - swift cover, layouts, Avi Gvili at Boulevard Books - easy, thorough publishing expertise.

Murray Weiss at Catalyst Literary Management - valuable initial honing of portions beyond any agent's normal involvement.

To casting directors and directors who individually/collectively took me into their creative families and for the multitude of collaborators in Hollywood - love and respect, perhaps most powerfully to those of you reprehensible and flawed.

Action Fans everywhere. *We who are about to die salute you.* Thank you for your thumbs up.

Marc Chancer at Activity Talent Agency – we did alright even if you've been an ineffectual cur for the last two decades.

Bobby Casimer, Tom Baughman, Gloria Kisel Hollis, James Andrew – decade spanning friendships.

To my sisters and brother who shared *upbringing* with me. You all know the glories and savageries. We're not victims, rather beneficiaries of a sterling heritage and environment.

To Ben and Sam, sons and mortal/immortal joy. Forgive me, choosing my truth rather than a kindlier Christian shuffle shirking of negativity. It is only because I don't believe in negativity as an enduring force.

Most adoringly Heidi Bright, forever and a day … incestuous Gretel to my stumbling Hansel as we pluck tidbits on the titillating stroll to love cottage. You've impacted every aspect of this as you have my life. Your aesthetic, stirring authenticity, relentless design drive, sexy proofing, each step and cuddle a redemptive tonic to a scoundrel's life.

I am not a moral man.

**"I never kill anyone above 5,000 feet." Vincent
Perotta / CRIMINAL MINDS**

*A musketeer appears, mincing steps from riverine mist, he
sets the barge afire...*

A party, a soiree. Stone arrived with a bevy of multiracial
sirens. I am tall, 6'2" on a good day, generally well spoken;
I know how to approach with politeness and presence.

"May I introduce myself?"

"You may", said Stone. I've admired his military service and entwined

foundational use of a multitude of story techniques –
animation, linear, non-linear, live action, flashbacks, superb
editing, sound etc. – NATURAL BORN KILLERS the
most arresting example. For a period, there were only a
handful of directors doing anything of 'importance', so
very few doing anything altering their age.

"My name is Patrick Kilpatrick. I'm a veteran of over one hundred
and fifty plus films and television shows as a lead actor.
I've worked with directors Antoine Fuqua, Guy Hamilton,
Chuck Russell, James Cameron, Nic Roeg. I'm a
screenwriter as well. I'd love to meet and discuss working
together."

I offered my card, discreet producer rectangle, tonally
harmonious to globally attractive business arts. A

6

communication far from the soft porn Vista Print so prolific with doomed aspiring actresses and actors.

"Of course!" said he. My trivial bonhomie mission … *inner monologue*, "Je suis enchante avec toi!" *Ollie speekie Frenchie!*

It's true (though not on my card) I'm a bruiser with my share of muscle and Scottish warrior DNA – body damaged, shuffled gaited, knuckle dragger linebacker façade overlaying 'Day of the Dead' skeletal failure in an intricately stitched Italian suit.

My personal attire is often superior to the 'movie wardrobe' I'm given before a film by the wardrobe department, so my own clothes *become* my dress in projects of limited means.

One must be refined yet arresting. An aura of Eastern Seaboard politeness and easy breeding in one's interactions indispensable for sure-fire effectiveness.

Not five minutes later, Stone was transformed. He had suck swallowed so much hooch his face was a lividly insane Jack O'Lantern, aneurysm features enflamed, mouth bellowing in a weightless, gravity free sphere, a late middle-aged member of a fracturing carnal conga line, slithering the boom boom room flanked by exquisite echelon floozie loveliness, card carrying & otherwise.

Only on one other occasion had I seen such rapidly deployed degenerative descent into alcohol poisoning.

'Cocktails' with actor Peter Greene – "Pulp Fiction" (Zed, the anal rapist), was similar.

You order vodka, he calls for a triple, has five in minutes, *a finger snap rude darling inebriate gesture to a woman*, then puking in the street, snorting shellfish laced vomit from his nostrils while borrowing your car keys to go buy crack.

Instantly I knew Stone would never remember me. C'est la vie - a cultural symptom, 'movie industry' networking warmth.

Three weeks later, I received a perturbed call from Stone's reportedly beautiful female assistant. "Why is your card in Oliver's pants?" She bit out, as if the sorcerer man and I might have groped each other in some damp, squalid men's room over bracing troughs of Colombiana snowflake in exchange for ... what?

Pale dissipated nut fluid emanating from flaccid members ... Ivy League savant grown haggard ...

I explained. She cut the call wordlessly, *another supplicant wastrel vaporized.* The perimeter for the barracuda director was secure – I joined other skinless shit birds flung shrieking into the blowhole.

Hollywood is a funny, schizophrenic playground. Timeless bodily sacrifice, accomplishment as a character actor will only provide you with respect in certain quarters.

Your turd for breakfast without a parking pass here, a near religious icon instilling sensory overload awe by noon there

… followed closely again with outlandish reverence, then second to split second insult within evening gatherings.

Large segments of the world's populace can hold one in transcendent fervor while industry studio 'other' extends no validation as a life form.

Nothing more than a salivating cog to the TOWN, no matter a god in Valhalla to people somewhere, anywhere, everywhere. The TOWN sees a trained beast: often not worthy of having one's cage swilled free of excrement without the asking … slice of flick flesh, flipped onto the floor awash with urea, dinner.

'They' – major agencies, studios, networks, have their pick over the party.

It's an unearthly dichotomy, somewhere beneath upper atmosphere superstar to the 'working man' philandering zones from which I crawl.

Greater the distance still from my American patriotic leanings to the Left Elitists Maoists of past and current Hollywood …

I arrived in Hollywood a Sons of the American Revolution, my ancestors having fought in nearly all major wars on the side of the American ideal.

Son of Yankee Connecticut and Rebel Virginia.

My own father received a Silver Star and Purple Heart at Okinawa in WWII. This school boy had embraced the civic, work and educational ethics of my mother and father, the towering moral and political force of Lincoln and the nobility, gravitas and acumen of Lee ... the wild flamboyance of Civil War Jeb Stuart ... the visual drama and justice of the Civil Rights Movement ... riots, battles, continental conquering ... all our shared mythology and origins, the rich and flawed perfection of freedom with self-sacrificial anti-authoritarianism.

As a university student I observed intensely as the party shamble revolution of the Viet Nam anti-war movement ravaged our national will, as Hanoi Jane reveled in betraying her country and was not held accountable, as Mr. Integrity Walter Cronkite sold inaccurate defeatist Tet and Khe San assumptions into living rooms nightly ... betrayals that with our withdrawal resulted in the massacre of two million South Vietnamese who valiantly fought on for freedom against cruelty and repression.

JFK's CIA assassination of Diem and Lyndon Johnson's wag the dog Gulf of Tonkin did not elude me.

"Remember the Maine" sent us to western hemisphere domination war against Spain, Teddy Roosevelt's not so covert seizure of the Panama Canal from Colombia, clever and right in the greater worldly good and manifest destiny of freedom.

Even the mixed bag of Guatemala, Chile ... Monroe Doctrine bitches ... we should expel Iran and China from South America now.

When we aided a nation's takeover, fostered coups or vanquished enemies in war, indigenous populations were served, business cultivated, private sector and religious impulses fostered, free speech and dollars flowed – choose your side motherfuckers, sprawling, expansive prosperity, roll up your sleeves and dance to the supremacy of the individual and the vote or align yourself with murderous collectivism – religious or otherwise - gone south, east, west, north into torture and murder. War is hell and let our decisive hell prevail or the world will be the worse for it.

Ask the people of Poland, Hungary, Yugoslavia, the Baltics, East Berlin, Japan, South Korea, Israel who they wish to triumph geopolitically. Take a poll among the peoples of the world to see where they wish to hang their immigrant aspirations, dissident disquiet and economic struggling to birth.

When I lay claim to a career in Hollywood, it was happening again as America and American armed forces men and women gave 50 million people the opportunity to vote in Iraq and Afghanistan against a vastly oppressive regime on the one hand and a murderous fundamentalist scourge on the other.

As we waged these two wars, the anti-military 'aid and comfort to our enemies' miasma turbulence about me was intolerable.

From an entire generation of Hollywood not one serves in Afghanistan or Iraq – indeed only five of us (myself among them) even visited the troops via USO during this period.

My being outnumbered was not justification for being silent.

I became the most outspoken and unrepentant *transgressive conservative* in all of Hollywood, have remained so for two decades.

First came my bone deep revulsion at the anti-American, anti-war bent of Hollywood …

Weapons constantly being placed in my hands for acting roles, I began to train with LAPD, the Special Investigative Service (SIS), Marine Recon and the Navy Seals.

I found I liked it. Tactics, the sport of it, rifles, pistols, combat shotguns, long distance sniping, urban carbines, close quarter battle, knives, caliber minutiae, pro law enforcement lingo and jargon … I was then continually witness to nonsense fee grubbing witless to weapon functionality gun control of California.

I awoke daily as an endangered species, a rational 'American' voice crowing and chortling in the winds of a Left enclave even pre-Fox News, a culture apparently insanely hell bent on not mere revisionism but abdication of the primary duty of government - safeguarding of the nation.

My eastern rambles would both groom me and set me apart from the specific culture and politics proliferating in Hollywood.

A distinct and true minority, I was and still am an American Patriot, steeped in history, war, and the encompassing rightness of my birth country.

I am the rarest of Hollywood creatures, simultaneously a decibel rich ribald actorini working and cavorting, while remaining utterly enamored with American exceptionalism.

A Libertine Patriot ...

One who believes we were right to be in Viet Nam, in Korea, Iraq, Somalia, Yemen and Afghanistan – fully. One who advocates both international isolation and regime change of state sponsored spree slayers, Saddam Hussein (hung appropriately), Kim Jong-Un (yet to suffer the fruits of his loathsome inherited legacy and present position), Ali Khamenei, Assad, Putin, Fidel (bugger made it to natural causes), Raoul, Nicolás Maduro (teetering), Ortega (on the brink), Xi Jinping and whomever else stands in the way of one person-one vote elected government.

Our American flaws are not imperialism or colonialism; rather we fail to put enough boots on the ground after invasion.

As rakish and cad-like as they come, *ever willing to tear love claw marks on any theatrical narcissist lover of every race, nationality, creed and political persuasion,* I still know *to the core* free people and governments everywhere should rise against dictators.

And we must embrace global democratic coalition partners – *and their citizens with whom I readily fraternize fashionably and in public displays of affection in chi-chi five-star European bathrooms* - powerfully foster freedom and democracy in the void.

My embrace of America, North and South, East and West, *Hollywood* even with my own adulterous prancing and mischief is an exultant spiral of pride and historical reverie.

We did indeed steal the state and town in which I reside from Mexico. Perhaps it is divine karma sending the Left Coast back to resembling something like the border towns of Tijuana and Juarez with ghettos of eternally gentrifying Silicon Beach bistros and astronomically priced pied-a-terre pocket residences.

Soaring culinary/cocktail energy and political insanity ...

Politicos in D.C. and Sacramento did nothing save treason, self-serve greed, rising myopic minarets of corrupt privilege, the electorate seethes. And thus, the hilariously appropriate rise of Trump.

*****

Has my outspoken political mindset affected my career?

Pervasive Hollywood values are sheep like and shallow, hardly deeply held, masquerading benevolence with nasty repressive views.

I cavort about the ditzy Hollywood maypole as minority reporter.

They don't call up and say, "Patrick we're not giving you this network show because you're politically aberrant."

For my sins I am recently typecast (institutional TV/film, not so in independent sprawl) as the go-to actor when they need towering white Aryan Supremacy, or a Serbian genocide war criminal.

Then again, other actors, husbanding their 'brand', can be notoriously hesitant to tackle the wretched antagonist side of the cinema fence. I may be getting my due for dramatic fearlessness.

Negative is difficult to measure; punishment for variants of thought not identified or quantified.

Rationality (mine) has finished friendships, conjured challenge of bodily harm, disrupted parties as hyperventilating hostesses (to the point of requiring EMT care and removal from the venue) spin about rooms like ensnared bats if one simply fails to equate Bush and Trump with Slobodan Milosevic and the anti-Christ.

The positive side of clear thinking and living is certainly real, firsthand knowledge of America beyond the coasts ... out from a system of thought as rigid as that which pigeonholes us all, typecasts everyone.

Those of us who know America as the illumination of the world, we're wondrous in our imaginings and connective tissue to liberty.

*****

Hollywood a mere three generations ago - dozens of stars of both sexes gave up status and opulence often to place their lives in mortal peril in aid to their country in wartime.

Jimmy Stewart, Eddie Albert, Charles Durning, Johnny Carson, Audrey Hepburn, Henry Fonda, Hedy Lamar, Bea Arthur and Marylyn Monroe - the list impressive, tribal.

The cinema factory of the forties, fifties into the sixties turned toward the fight against tyranny to create dreams bolstering the American ideal.

To the contrary, Hollywood, in my entire life beyond adolescence, offered safe harbor to geopolitical evil, adversaries of freedom by a 'compassionate' anti-American Frankenstein anatomy.

Viet Nam through to this very second, Hollywood has heeled over like a runaway garbage galley, rigging and rudder shot away, drifting and belching sulfuric ideological fumes (beyond any benign inclusion of middle country patriotic Americans with diversely critical views) to become a full-blown septic contagion of anti-democratic rhetoric.

Failure of BLACK HAWK DOWN to receive any consequential Academy Awards.

Shit-for-brains racial murder criticism of AMERICAN SNIPER arises from the Left when that flick *finally* emerges to 'absolve' Clint Eastwood – complete cinema void of pro-American films during 2 wars by our finest

16

directors - FLAGS OF OUR FATHERS, LETTERS FROM IWO JIMA & the whitewashing puerile, shallow and corrupted HOOVER.

AVATAR depicts US Marines as destroyers of the environment – and indeed the 'Tree of Life' - instruments of corporate murder of native 'people of color'. This at the very moment these warriors – who've bled for freedom for two hundred and fifty years - were rescuing tens of thousands in hurricane ravaged Haiti.

These movies deserved to be made but must be questioned as calculated propaganda when not a single pro-American film emerges from 12 years of war.

Gay rights, racial diversity, gender equality – real liberation issues mirroring the evolving American experience … advocacy of these, *even work for their realization* is still not a pass for anyone unless victimhood is bestowed on everyone. Within Hollywood embrace of every weirdly contrived matrix of ideas is required. Minimal common sense is transformed to reactionary Nazism and misogyny.

Ill-liberal fashionable snot is flung wide – Hollywood Dem partisan hypocrisy, sanctuary city criminality, feminist ideology is aligned with international jihadi oppression of women, diminishment of fathers/men becomes the norm, a step over others race to divvy loot with China (ruthless one-party autocrats) the order of the day, violent suppression of discourse and nouveau cinematic puritan constraint in the name of 'discomfort' levels … all emboldened to Alice in Wonderland terror by plucked-from-thinnest-air words and concepts – white privilege, SIS males, reparations, unconscious patriarchy, hate speech, *Resist*!

What's a Libertine Patriot to do but seek fairness, pleasure and justice at every twisting labyrinth, to counter perversity of 'compassion' or 'values'.

Look down the governmental and societal road and try to spot the long con.

*****

The short con - division and discord, long con perhaps control and destruction of America. The shadow of anti-democracy is advancing even as life and sumptuous light and opportunity is everywhere.

Moment by moment we seek freedom – chosen individually and collectively even as division is foisted upon us every day.

Courage is a choice, freedom is a choice, happiness is a choice, evolution is a choice – and personal accountability the only standard – take the miracle results of life as they are shoved at you and revel in the feast.

Pendulum and upheaval … Hollywood remains a lavish conversational high stakes enclave. But only if counter voices come forward.

Out here arterial village shrill screeching bleeding over the exercise of American Power in any form has fatally weakened Hollywood's influence – a precipitous erosion of at least 2 decades. One would be hard pressed to discern this fall unless one actually traipsed among the diverse states of great America.

One must continually take up colorful semaphore emblazoned with patriotic/altruistic imagery to wend the wayward financial and social agendas.

Long ago it became far finer to be an American with grasp of history … a brave human superseding the 'proper' Hollywood advocacy, to stand before those ripping the fabric of American life – an industry swarm dancing on a burnt umber shit heap of hypocrisy.

*****

I crawl in an odd no man's coliseum.

One is a 'Savior' simply because you have appeared in ANYTHING. ANYTHING has an eternal life because of DVD, VOD, cable HBO, SHOWTIME, IFC, streaming NETFLIX, HULU, AMAZON, unending replay round the world. ANYTHING has value simply because it was made at all.

On the other hand, if the very movies of your generation could not have been made without your ilk - your own stunts, rewriting unknowing and poorly conceived scripts (oblivious to true artistry, lacking awareness of the collective media betterment and global business acumen), creating your own memorable lines, elevating every project and deeply human fallen star 'name'.

19

Emerge like young Brando by comparison …

It *matters literally and greatly* if one has left body parts and psychic pieces in astonishing, caffeine-fueled effort on each day of eighteen-hour work – eluding slipping toward professional euthanasia.

I am simultaneously 'Legend' and political pariah to an institutional Death Star – both sides of a ridiculous paradigm.

I have few illusions and no lack of self-esteem. I am a champion, Broadway, off-Broadway, every soap, have been catapulted from PBS to Spielberg (he called my agent, no audition, not even a meeting prior to first day principal photography), Los Angeles Theater Center with Academy Award winner Tony Richardson and Richard Olivier (son of Sir Lawrence), James Cameron's and Jerry Bruckheimer's premier forays into TV, *merely the beginning.*

I set, hold the world's record for guest star TV spots in a concentrated period – 27 episodes on 18 different shows, *more episodes in a year than any series main actor on a single series* … and I competed for nearly all, sometimes read 2, 3 times per.

And that was only part of the rigorous trip. In the same year, four studio movies, four independent projects – writing scripts and raising children, couch surfing with LA friends to pay for the immaculate black bottomed pool cul de sac best school district house in Santa Barbara to shelter youngsters and then wife.

Sixty-two TV titles, 76 films, 13 projects in development, 7 in post and climbing, countless actors mentored at universities, throughout the City of Angels, USA and overseas.

I did it without a major agency, without PR team.

I am an entertainment warrior by any measure, simply by longevity itself – on the side of continuous crucible as a lead in the finest international action films and television.

But I am a peon, a peasant picking up potatoes in a field.

There is little brotherhood in TOWN – no BAND OF BROTHERS bond, no shared existential memory beyond PR –and yes, copious swaths of self-interest, jockeying for lateral and ascending position and scoring.

Without bitterness, we are all simple and intricate fodder for the 'culture of theft' … ceaseless stealing of intellectual property by major agencies and production companies.

Whatever real friendship and leadership exists must be cultivated by deep, continuing suicidal example, for the wildlife in this kingdom knows no sense and sensibility of intrinsic connection.

I glimpsed Stone last in a documentary about a true Hollywood creative, screen scribe/director/gleeful politically incorrect raconteur John Milius (APOCALYPSE NOW, CONAN, DIRTY HARRY and RED DAWN but a few). An inspiring gaggle of Hollywood luminaries: Coppola, Eastwood and Michael Mann, Lucas, Dreyfuss and Kathleen Kennedy came together to celebrate Milius, for his King Kong manhood and literate lug humanity, his prolific workmanship and irreverent individualism, a life lived well boldly. A man with elephant guns in his Paramount office and blond cigars the size of Viking phalluses.

Steeping the ironic poignancy, ultimate teller of storylines and spiels Milius is rearing back from a muting stroke.

Stone whined like a gap-toothed, slimed carney barker, mouthing ideological hits and slurs with the graceless negativity of a Cultural Revolution acolyte – at someone for whom he should have held simpatico warmth no matter political divergence. But no, humorless and pussified, Hitler upper lip jazz dot moustache prominent, he piddled and winced in the manner of Hollywood 'maturity', stabbing Milius's 'blunted political growth'.

In Hollywood and Stone's hyena sunset, if one cherishes views or lives empowered by trite patriotism, even lampooning in any way apart from anti-orthodoxy, then one has 'failed to evolve' or 'wallowed in juvenility' as Stone purports is the case for 'reactionary' Milius.

*****

Hollywood culture - superficially benign, vision/no vision hedonist, obsession/allure/hack craft centered ... a vortex barely misted by true America – giving off caustic insidious national cynicism, creating citizen castrati, full flush rolling into generation after generation of blunted children and a poisoned body politic.

Despite a lifetime of Hollywood, nothing is as it seems.

We all stray. Our flaws are our own.

One vacates one's self from the Los Angeles scrabble, the often-senseless repetition of audition and availability at one's own peril.

Or not, by exile then ascend.

Relentless introduction of new talent, pinball shortness of the collective entertainment and audience memory, failure to leave loyalty behind and leap from one agency to another at that pristine moment of timing, personal demons, politics and bad habits, age – all can conspire to topple *or perversely catapult* the career house of labor and cards.

It is a glorious, lacerating, at times grace infused and repellent life.

I recently did a film with an FBI Middle East field investigator, a woman who sifts among the body parts of children for evidence, hunts, incarcerates and causes Al Qaeda murderers to be incinerated by drone and Spec Op raids. There is a price on her head.

When I told her of our lives in Hollywood she said in wonder, "How can you exist in a world where you trust no one?"

I smiled – "Knowing full well you may be betrayed, just as you Dear Lady operate."

Acting, as healing journey, has allowed me to corral dark impulses and thoughts necessary to perform villainy … name it and claim it, as 'bad guy' I have purposefully cultivated sidewalks of genocide, child cannibalism, ruthless cowardice, power mad ballroom psychic sashaying, the flaying of flesh and decorum, slicing raw 'cross all law and taste' … for the sake of cinematic antagonism.

I am grateful.

None of us come from nowhere.

I came to life as I might say 'exuberant'- a self-congratulatory assessment carrying charm. The sort of self-rationalization that in the hands of a gifted stratospheric CLOCKWORK ORANGE 'playa' could be used to facilitate all manner of delicious behavior:

Pubescent gas station robbery and shop lifting sprees …

Prep school cock groping a slumbering roommate and preemptively 'bearing false witness' against the sleeper …

Plucking ruby pearled virginity from skittish flocks of en pointe nymphets at American Ballet Theater …

Poaching newly-wed tourist wives in St. Bart's amidst local inbred French Sicilian-like chinless ginger 'tards …

Statutory 'rape' on Saba (renowned scuba mecca) …

LIFE Magazine media creative marathons on mescaline…

Injected cocaine sessions on international fashion shoots –
filthy, sweating, near death …

Feigned epileptic seizures to escape Long Island Sound
sandbar transgender dating …

Violently body guarding Jimi Hendrix (and every other
rock group & singer holding forth in the day) with New
York Jets …

Summarily fired from Playboy as copy hack and four hours
later persuading preeminent magazines (including Christian
funded periodicals) to pay in advance for hang gliding and
cocaine war journalistic assignments in Chile, Venezuela
and Colombia …

Amorality, burn the candle at both ends intemperance,
drug experimentation, observation, piracy and literacy …
pillars sustaining Hollywood since Edison stole George
Melies A TRIP TO THE MOON imagery vision at the
dawn of the 20th century.

Where else would an energetic, sex addict psychopath
slither? It's Hollywood or Washington – TINSEL TOWN
chicks superficial and less brainy, the weather finer, *less
humid* – and gluttonous swag won't send you to Federal
prison.

*Presidents and Congress have their own manners of
slurping from the gifting suite.*

Prior to lunging into Hollywood's vacuous and exalted
kaleidoscopes, I had parents, sisters and a brother, a

childhood athletic and terrifying, enriched, searing and saucy.

Origin, era, our before-womb-genetics and individual nature fuse – a propelling hybrid of scars and abilities, debilitating weakness & unlimited potential.

Tell you how a man devotes his life to imaginary thugs, killers, serial rapists, corrupt and ruthless hit men, racists, bullies and bank robbers, damaged, violated souls?

I will illuminate.

I will morph considerably, have my arc, from sexual scamp into a singular Movieland voice of common sense and Old Glory 'virtues', love of God, country … prodigal American experiment - and I will not only survive, but thrive in Los Angeles and its bastion of mad Leninism … sprinkle dust Hollywood.

Let's start where starts start.

Bang the gong!

The arsonist grenadier retreats after quaffing from the goblet.

- Patrick Kilpatrick / September 18, 2018

The Devil whispers in italics.

One: Genesis

"People need to understand fear. Do you understand fear? Do you?" Robert Carlson / BABYLON 5

I was born backwards, sign of the warlock, Ellie Faye Hine's umbilical cord crushing my throat, first moments like a pink suckling piglet strangled by a slim purple bloody python.

The doctor yanked me abruptly from her womb, mauling my nose exiting the offering pelvis. Descended from venturing across the sea to Virginia English Protestants (between 1607 Jamestown and 1620 Plymouth Rock), irascible American Revolutionary patriots, slave holding stalwarts, defeated Southern Confederates, Quakers, a rail road track sweeper rising to Great Depression engineer father and a suffragette teacher mother, she endured, gave birth and aspired for herself and her children to points beyond madness.

She was 21, already an acclaimed college graduate, married to a young war hero with a national baseball reputation, a 7th grade teacher whose Virginia job interviews were scheduled purely to ascertain that she was not a Jew – Hines rather than Heinz.

My mother through my poetic prism and a lifetime infuriated by her, avoiding her, living and churning as a child within her conflict of mental illness, making my sole goal to not parent as she did, *to not become her in manner or effect*, I offer her DNA, her cerebral intricacies -

Defeated Rebel glory imbued with hunger for
imagined/real white American revolutionary glamor and
grandeur of place and station ... her fallen Southern
stature, a seething insult to the very core of her pioneer
nobility at onetime carving riches from a diseased
wonderland of frontier and mortal sacrifice, then slavery
made over into art and entitlement. All of it – all taken by
rapine vermin Yankee imperialists, rabble of the unwashed
and unholy, her full-frontal fifties psyche further sold on
the chopping block of perfectionism, half lucid vehemence
and chemical imbalance.

"Hello – the boy has a way with words". Indeed, it was the earliest and easiest way to keep her from beating me. Come up with a new phrase, a metaphor, a simile – "This wildflower looks like that one's eyes, that car jiggles like Jane's belly button when she laughs'.

She was mad as a hatter with the cunning of the diseased and disenfranchised, compelled to overcome and rip.

I was told by my mother, in a subsequent year, the physician in attendance at my birth lost his license for alcohol abuse.

Let me say this loudly and clearly: information and opinion conveyed by my mother is the subject of her ongoing self-interest and revisionism. While she is a person of high intelligence, insight and general good will somewhere, these attributes are always shaded by derangement and conflicting agenda. Her historical coloring book is a well spring of self-aggrandizement, guilt and spin, enthused by certain mental misfiring.

There is no way of knowing whether his 'alleged' drunkard nature caused the hapless failure to simply sculpt my shattered but momentarily malleable newborn nose. In any case I was born with a mashed, mixed martial artist's countenance, into a world of physical trauma, flailing for air and life.

It would seem an easy leap to say Faye endured her own share of stressed agony during this spectacle in a one-room clinic in Orange, Virginia.

After months of false labor, she had gone for seven days in a row to the tiny medical station expecting the turmoil to end.

Perhaps this accounts for some of her stellar difficulty with me, her future homicidal inclinations, her physical, verbal and emotional lashings, snap hot personality voids and vortexes, all the while tripping toward some exhausted delusional well-wishing amongst her own truly realized accomplishments.

Nine months before my arrival on her honeymoon in Virginia Beach, VA, she had been fitted with a birth control diaphragm by a doctor with his office over a theater. (Overtly symbolic given one of my future professions.)

Adamant to *not* become pregnant, despite the diaphragm, she and my father conceived me in the Gay Manor Hotel *(really,* amusingly foreshadowing historic/contemporary sexual proclivities of theater and entertainment - professions absorbing me for much of a lifetime).

Four children and eleven years later she discovered her uterus was tilted, the diaphragm permanently useless from the very moment it entered her body.

(Presumably – one should never presume - she extracted the diaphragm for the actual births. Who knows if this story she relayed to me as justification for her outbursts is even true.)

With each accidental pregnancy she grew more insane, overwhelmed, still made due, went on with work in a forged alchemy of driven anger, expanding personal rigidity, residual racism and religious separatism, real-life/ inner chaos.

Oxygen deprivation from prolonged compression of the mother-to-fetus lifeline may have caused me permanent neurological damage. Faye's smoking mentholated KOOLs throughout my gestation *could have contributed* adversely to the miracle.

I'm laughing now - her smoking is the first instance of a reoccurring theme of paradox environment in my sojourn on earth. I will often find myself the odd bubbly

Tasmanian Devil set down in an environment directly at odds with my spirit.

Why would the universe plop an asthmatic air desperate pupa into the arms of a chain smoker?

Why deliver a delicate into the hands of a volatile banshee?

Why an allergy riddled colostrum seeking babe to a battle for survival with a bottle feeder on the border of maniac town?

We plummet through startlingly phosphine atmosphere without heat shield, tiles flinging off, exposing soft hopelessly vulnerable cores ready for incineration.

Injury to my brain and skull also may have occurred due to accelerated passage of my baby head through Faye's vaginal cage. In contrast, a baby going through labor in the head-down position usually experiences gradual molding (temporary reshaping of the skull) over the course of a few hours.

Researchers have identified a relationship between breech birth and autism. I seem to have avoided this complication though there are acquaintances that deem me mentally mangled - expansive unfiltered vocab, hyper exhilaration, galloping risk behavior, up-tempo anti-authoritarianism … unruly shit eating cowboy grin over hulking earthy lurching tenderness lacquered with Louis X1V debauchery.

Get a grip Patrick!

Years later, when I was seducing a rebirther woman of exquisite beauty and large hips, she pronounced my entrance to planet earth as clear precursor to my life.

In her validation model of her life's work, I was born clawing for survival, railing against physical hurdle to my very being and triumphing over that challenge. She proclaimed I would repeat this over and over again … thus self-creating passages through playing with fire youth, motorcycle and auto wrecks, violent sports, war correspondence, layered unrepentant promiscuity, drugs and infidelity, acting and writing - *whip up one's life by any means, then not die but thrive!*

They named me on the pale cream birth certificate for my father, Robert Donald Kilpatrick, Sr., - albeit Jr. – 11:33am arrival, August 20th, '49, but for convenience I was Pat from day one.

Father was Robert, father was Bob. I wasn't ever Bobby. I became without calculation or legal name change Patrick Kilpatrick, social security card, age 13, driver's license, age 16, marriage certificate and passport, land, cars, my twenties – as prophetic and psychologically fulfilling a moniker as ever conjured.

My birth wouldn't be the last experience I had struggling against asphyxiation. I was born with fierce asthma, convulsing throat and lungs.

I was allergic to everything – meat, mold, horses, cats, rabbits, eggs, milk. I was not expected to live, much less be bountiful. Is it any wonder my mother was driven to unbalance struggling to keep me alive, carrying me to specialist after medical specialist?

I was not breast fed, but by bottle, fashion of the 'modern' post-war era, *kiss off* primary colostrum ... no rich nipple milk of antibodies and immunoglobulin, which shields newborns as they wander into our world of bacteria and viruses.

The medicines for asthma in those days were all based on stimulating the body's adrenals, essentially, I was given speed. These elixirs stopped the attack but wound me up exponentially. Adrenal depletion by exhilarated force has been a lifelong love affair.

Through nights, for years, my father would hold me in his arms, pacing ceaselessly, whispering endearments, "I love you Pat, yes I do", over and over, as I gasped for life itself. Then at last, plump and cherubic, I was whisked by my mother to doctor conventions, held aloft by physicians as a bonny trophy, a squirming, tickled symbol of fleshy chuckles, the will and skill to live.

Two: Papa Power

"These kids are your ticket outta here buddy. Cops won't make a move as long as they're here." Paul Masters / SHARK

My first and most profound images of you father: a 6'6", 250 lb. giant on the baseball mound, blazing forth as a pitcher. You would survey the arena of the field, taking in the base runner's slyly bold, tantalizing intentions for base theft, all of us awash in the brisk chatter speech dancing about the diamond.

Gazing back to the catcher with the dark piercing examination of an artist jeweler selecting facets of a gem to be precisely exorcised … those arms rising upward and arcing back, slinging forward, the ball igniting to fire and then devilishly slicing this way and that before the flailing batter. I know your visual and genetic mythology as if it were my own, for it is mine, given by you.

After a game, you would lie in a rugged canvas hammock, a relic of Navy service, massive forearms tanned by the summer sun, curved forearm hairs gone red golden … sleeping the peace that comes from post-athletics and surviving combat. The day would move away, heat distilling, transmuting to the cool of evening.

Years later I would move closer and pour Tabasco Sauce or ground graham cracker down your open mouth.

Gagging, choking you would explode from the hammock, enraged with the insult, driven wild by life assault.

I would turn and flee, confident in my agile youth to escape Zeus … the glory - to tempt God in his repose, to force each Higher Power into lethal notice and futile pursuit. Assured that within ten yards the Deity himself would be overtaken by laughter just as I am now convulsed by the youth and irreverence of my own sons.

Life and acting are this very ceremony, wickedly pouring crumbs and hot sauce down the throat of life, waiting for explosion and exhilarations.

Very young, when I experienced severe growing pains in the night, you would rub my legs endlessly, liberating me from pain just as you had attempted to free my breathing, crooning bits of songs I carry with me always. I have conveyed my tune to my boys – singing "Angel from Montgomery" to your grandsons, and they remember love as well.

You, this remarkable man, a guiding tower of male behavior, descended from resolute Scotch Irish and American fighters, born to a Louisiana farming couple, willed yourself to become the finest scholar athlete of your high school. After the attack on Pearl Harbor, you turned away from several college athletic scholarships, joined the Navy at 18.

It was near your death, large man numbed by morphine, that I asked and was told what you had done in the war…

36

Impossibly brave, you fought in North Africa, Sicily and across the Pacific the entire war, received a battlefield commission and swam to hyper violent, pestilence ridden islands before the Marines as a 'Beach Jumper' - a tandem unit to the Underwater Demolition Teams (UDT), legendary precursor to the Navy SEALS.

How different you all were from modern Navy Seals, not armored up with max firepower, you and your lads were simply boys in khaki shorts, stroking the bloody water to war.

You received a Silver Star and Purple Heart while clearing obstacles and mines in the water and on the black sand of Iwo Jima and night missions to Okinawa.

Half your unit was killed, young bodies decimated, not one escaped being grievously wounded – your Lieutenant mortally wounded in a first volley you picked up his .45, shot a screaming Jap 3 times in the chest just as he stabbed your thigh through with his bayonet.

Then you rose and led the survivors back over their own wired explosives to safety …

"It was like the Civil War", you uttered near the end, huge body laid low by bone marrow cancer and heart failure, your eyes wide, illuminated with pain. "We fought with sticks and coconuts and knives."

How different from the *historical* voice you took up at table throughout our young lives to offer us broad strokes of the Pacific, dazzling effortless gravitas, your 'Cronkite' voice.

At the impending moment of death, you were back with those boy combat swimmers who did not come home. You did not see yourself as any kind of hero, rather you nearly wept at the loss of those left behind.

I imagine those that survived, honed by combat and victory, matured physically and mentally, and returning to be educated on the G.I. Bill, taking to athletic fields as MEN, like no generation before them.

As captain of the University of Richmond baseball team, you struck out George Herbert Walker Bush (captain of Yale) to win the national collegiate baseball championship. For a period you held the record for most games won by a single collegiate pitcher. A contract offer to join a NY Yankees farm team came to you.

To serve your family (my mother's wishes) you turned away from the mythic diamond, began first as math teacher and coach, then as lowly insurance underwriter for a company in Hartford, Connecticut.

Faye having dated your pitching teammate Lew Burdette (not your collegiate pitching equal, later perhaps the greatest World Series pitcher of all time – winning epically three games against the Yankees {twice on shutouts} in 1957) believed ball players to be an uneducated lot. True enough Lew was booted from University of Richmond for 'scholastic delinquency'.

I would have dumped her, ejected any woman who turned me away from the Yankees.

The Korean War called my father back into the Navy – again as UDT. I spent age one to six in Virginia Beach, VA, eastern proto-surfer town. UDT didn't invade North Korea. He described this service as "killing Virginia sharks with hand grenades".

*****

At two I made my first police blotter appearance, became object of a citywide law enforcement dragnet. I wandered to a municipal sewer 23 blocks away from our apartment home in a white 3-piece shorts suit - Little Lord Fauntleroy, *early sartorial Tom Wolfe un autre Virginian - even then attention to wardrobe -* climbed/plummeted down a manhole and into the labyrinth drain system. My attire became sopping brown. I was rescued three hours later when a passing woman heard my little voice singing "Jesus loves me". Angels delivering me from shit storms in the netherworld.

At the same tender age, I scaled out of my crib, went out the 2nd story window, clung by my fingers on the ledge for two hours earnestly cooing over and over, "Please God give me strength!"

My parents, a Navy party downstairs, *rollicking the high balls,* and their guests marveled at this cute divinity evocation till they climbed the stairs in tipsy mass to say goodnight, discovering the gripster hanging. A woman – who was she? - rushed forward to seize me back from free fall splatter.

Bodily wounds and began - my left hand carries deep interesting scimitar scars where I sliced it open running/falling on a sidewalk with a glass of water.

In a black and white pic from the period I'm a platinum blond smiling blocky tot on a mystery beach – ebullient all boy mischief maker with a mid-twenties, strikingly tall slim chiseled aquiline nosed, dark haired father, arm in arm with his one year out of college wife, new mother, Susan Hayward tresses, shapely in pin up one-piece bathing suit.

They were an 'American' post-war couple carved as children by unimaginable economic eruption and worldwide triumphant conflict.

In another photo, I'm a *tiny* make-believe cowboy – *captured just as many thousands of children 'cross the country were by roaming shutterbugs* … cap guns, fleece lined chaps, fringed vest, steadfast and sturdy pinto pony, sparkling tack and saddle - *wardrobe and props, camera ready* - beyond pleased to be mounted and ready to gallop real and conjured realms.

Three: More Brain Damage

"You're One Chromosome Away From Being a Monkey." Dallas Adler / NCIS: LOS ANGELES

My first fully realized narrative memory came suddenly four days after my fifth birthday. Inaugural day of kindergarten I was vibrating with joy. We tikes took to the tiny baseball diamond outside the school. I remember ecstatic spin dancing in the sun, next at bat. I whirled about in goofball exhibitionism, swinging wide the miniature warm-up bat, feeling genetically the entire catechism of national pastime moves – a reverie of hallucinatory light.

There was a brilliant interplanetary flash of white and gold, then sickening vertigo and vibration. I had tootled from on deck circle into batter's box, just as another pre-school hitter took a full, shoulder high bludgeoning swing. The bat connected crack force with my right eyebrow (thank God not my nose), and the impact had instantly opened my skull with a wide, deep gash.

Blood cascaded into my eyes, across my face, over my neck, chest and shirt. I staggered a bit, little pain but acute, shocking disorientation.

Those teachers not sickened by the outpouring of blood scurried to help me. There was a stampede of revulsion and screaming chaos – image pieces of people's slacks or shirts, faces and eyes, skin, cheeks and jowls, thin legs all I could discern as the fearful fled or milled mindlessly about, creatures unable to deal with the bloodletting.

My mother was immediately called by school authorities. We lived minutes from the school, she was soon there.

Faye was wonderfully distraught, enraged, default raving roiling with the natural maternal fear she felt for me. She ordered me to load myself into the forest green '54 Pontiac. By then, I had several blood drenched towels soiling the car's seat. Lashing out at me tearfully, she squealed the vehicle away in donuts of dust from the school field toward the nearby hospital.

For the moment, I was gleefully happy. I leaned against the passenger seat door, taking in my mother's reaction, a sly, secret smile on my young face. Like an emerging professional, stunned by his own dexterity, I was intrigued by the attention to me for recklessness. The rich anguish and dazzling discomfort this created in my mother far out stripped any pain. I soon received 23 internal and 27 exterior stitches in the emergency room. I began carrying a lifelong jagged scar within the right eyebrow.

After the hospital and a piece of candy as conciliatory reward, she took me home and bathed me in the sink of the blood patina. The entire female cheerleading squad of the high school where she was the girls' athletic coach, sweater breasts & mid-calf skirted legs over kitchen chairs, sat about adoring the cute little towhead with war wound bandages and sudsy lathered up genitalia. I splashed and stomped my stocky little boy legs in watery revelation - baby vaudeville before belles.

Four: Culinary Bits

"Somebody got sloppy and attracted a Witch." Death / CHARMED

My boyhood was as rarified as it was eruptive … a turbo literate, well-fed war zone replete with paradoxical violence and reoccurring nightmares … Arcadian landscapes, whippings with Hoover vacuum cleaner chords … mop handle beatings with skull stitches.

A few years ago, after starring in the film PARASOMNIA as an eloquent serial killing mesmerist, I shaved my head and the L shaped scars remained a half century later.

May god have mercy on those - <u>including studio operational director producer wonks</u> - who know nothing of ON THE WATERFRONT, HOFFA cruelty of the movie street biz. Their scars will remain forever as well. PARASOMNIA was directed by dear friend Bill Malone (FEAR.COM, HOUSE ON HAUNTED HILL) and he would nearly lose his house, his chick, get his ass handed to him in distribution and remain saddled with debts, including $17k to yours truly.

The Korean 'police action' – perhaps history's greatest sanitizing jargon - in Asia over, father packed pretty, already overwhelmed and angry 'rebel' wife and child (by then joined by two sisters) and went north to 'yellow-bellied rape Yankeeland' for noble low insurance job.

My mother seethed with resentment at leaving her family in Richmond, Virginia. He promised to haul her back to her state. A pact that was kept thirty years later. By then, consistently bitching, she railed at the return.

My father and mother chose to isolate us from expanding suburban/urban Hartford blight (*Nigrahs on the march*) on a Connecticut farm in Litchfield County, a quintessential New England postcard expression in the northwest corner of the state.

He drove to work 60 miles each way in an original VW Beetle - incongruous with his bulk. On more than one occasion he rolled the iconic Hitler clown car on icy roads – doing interchange loop to loop on the hustle to Bradley Field airport – a large white lab rat in an auto ball – and always walked away unscathed.

My mother worked as well, strove heroically toward graduate higher education and material ascendancy.

She wasn't designed for 'stay at home'. A succession of kindly black and Italian nannies built me kites, ethnic cuisine and daily humanity. I was happiest when mother was off-site –- getting her not one but two Masters degrees and a gym teacher post - she was clearly unfathomably raving.

Her work became reprieve from fits, hurled epithets - *bugger, bastard, worthless* – tense vibrational artillery barrages that ushered in my nightmares of homicidal pursuit.

Dark dreams intermingled with true scourges and false
bigotries of my age – Samurai sword wielding sadistic
Japanese torturers, screaming after me to castrate and
behead me running as a Catholic priest in the jade
Philippine jungle with a coitus worthy movie star, panting,
petrified together until we plunge off a cliff, falling miles. I
smash awake hitting the floor beside my bed. sodden with
sweat, guilty, fearful of being 'caught' for unknown crimes.

Each night Faye's screams or stillness were out there in the beyond of the house.

Work, while hardly extinguishing her dementia, at least provided daytime hours with her rage elsewhere.

Of course, as a child one both knows instinctually this isn't the way things should be and also assumes and absorbs this is the natural course of things. One repeatedly looks for ways in which to love, rationalize, excuse while becoming ever more terror packing.

My first scorching sexual model and mad mistress of the erotic mind chamber was my mother of course – field hockey firm, Rita Hayworth devastating.

Like many boys I fantasized about my mother. There was no one else for miles in the country and she was undeniably evocative picking mint in the garden bending and flexing in a mismatched bikini, panties from one set, bra from another.

We didn't call the place organic, didn't even know the word. My insurance executive Dad with recreational gentleman farmer aspirations that ushered him back to his Louisiana bayou roots would never have fed our horses, cattle, chickens, sheep, anything but fine grain and seed, pure hay and water.

Traditional upwardly mobile gentry animals roamed the land (along with a single egg producing chicken) … chewed grasses, gnawed tree bark, gobbled fallen crab apples, pecked and rolled in Yankee soil, drank from streams that rushed in spring and slowed to nearly stagnant dry carve trickles by August end.

I reared a Black Angus bull from small calf to two-year old perfection in 4-H pastoral pageantry - ribbons, pies and carnival rides.

Winter mornings, sheet ice nights, summer dawn and dusk, frost spring and Indian summer fall, I fed Fudgy from a nipple bucket filled with powdered milk I churned. Moving on I grained, watered and hayed our sheep flock, horses and ponies.

Fudgy behaved like a dog, following behind me in the hills of Robin Ridge Farm, named because hundreds of the red breasted aviators flared in each spring.

Every few feet the young bull would nudge me with his snout, letting me know he was there.

For my younger toddler brother, this was dangerous affection. Fudgy's moist nose became a propelling flipper hurling David high into the air, arc slamming the small boy to the ground.

When I jumped pole & beam fences on our hunter horses Fudgy followed, tucking his short legs up under his barrel body and miraculously clearing the fence. Tickled I threw a halter over his muzzle, saddled him up with an enormous western saddle rig.

I went jumping, improbable and wonderful. His limit was 2 1/2 feet, never attempting the 5-6 feet at the outer edge of my colliding mass human horse competitions on mile long speed steeplechase courses. When Fudgy hit two years old a single man came for him. I watched as the teenage bull reared, toppling backward, flailing his strong neck, not wanting to go up the truck ramp. I was eleven and that was the way I had been raised. Not to feel or question, not even to know the question.

Four days later, with family, I ate the finest steak I have ever had – 'feed five kids and two adults' Angus marbled slabs as large as stingrays.

*****

My mother would attempt to butcher me in the dead of night.

I was awakened by Faye wailing, walls reverberating with blows. Halted by my father in the hallway, she was only feet away, struggling to reach me with a large 'Alfred Hitchcock' psycho kitchen blade.

My gentle, mammoth Under Water Demolition Team Navy father was forced to throttle her about the throat, pinning her against the wall, pleading, "STOP FAYE, STOP FAYE, STOP!!!!" Finally slapping her cheek hard as she beat him viciously with her hands and feet. At the impact of his hand, her face and body seized, shocked rigid, she collapsed in swooned release, a string cut puppet, wet eyed, babbling on the floor. He picked her up and carried her away.

Resembling an un-killable demonic resurrected movie villainess she came for me repeatedly day and night.

What would drive a mother to attempt to kill her child? I'm not sure there is an answer - a sensible reply from a tangled mind. I was - not yet old enough to know it - a seedling adversary, a source of questioning aliveness assaulting her lattice of control.

My father once said, "Your mother cannot say she is sorry and she's fiercely rigid. Dangerous qualities."

*****

Along our property lines, using early fence stretchers and staples, hand post-hole diggers when no four-hundred-year-old maples were in position to serve as fence pillars, father and I strung and maintained five strands of barbed wire in the enduring contest to keep our sheep captive.

Teamwork and purity of labor. Time, bonding, love.

Three strands will do for cattle, five will surely fail for sheep.

A wonderfully hapless task, wrangling of sheep, they 'fade' through fence lines, ever munching, placing one short mutton leg through the lower wire, then the next, always nibbling, barbs gliding through their thick oily coats, until voila, entire flock is now outside the wire ready to defy the shepherd ... like spilled mercury insolently laughing at the chemist, his thick, plump fingers desperate to funnel flowing silver into a bottle.

The fence line – my father and I carrying buckets and aluminum maple syrup harvesting hardware, drill and spouts, both in flannel shirts and khaki trousers over high muck out boots, spring air pure morning chill, warming, drilling one tree, tapping in spile, hanging the bucket on a cast clasp. Drops of clear, sometimes yellow amber beginning its rhythmic percussive descent. The first resonant *ping* on metal, then liquid upon deeper liquid, brimming bucket in short order.

What a thing this was, he and I hauling maple syrup sap together, along rushing spring white waterways and glade green new born each year forests, pouring the sweet into stainless steel milk cans, transporting them to a local farmer owning a 'sugar shack' distillery - boiling down to varying darkening shades and textures, ending in candy for a child. How lucky I am to have this with me.

Father executed a first squirrel in front of me when I was very young. Riddled the bushy in the back with shredding shotgun shot in violation of every youthful cowboy hero ethic. Stunning to me …

Medal winner at Okinawa slaying a small defenseless Disney creature.

Immunized against feeling –

I later slaughtered squirrels and rabbits by the hundreds. A forest ranger found me with dozens dead at my feet, heavy smoking double barrels slung in my easy grasp. I didn't eat them, didn't feed them to the dogs. Simple killing jubilation …

I had my own hobby military industrial complex "Frog Space Program". It was after all the dawn of American interplanetary imagination. Society and I were both enraptured with the race to the moon. With homemade rockets and captured frogs as astronauts – blasted skyward, parachuted back; they didn't do well with G-forces, their internal organs spilling from their slack slit cantaloupe mouths.

I 'tested' detonations – strapped amphibians to M80 firecrackers (essentially ¼ stick of dynamite) & cherry bombs to watch them dive to escape 'safety', *count the seconds,* the depth charge-like slime flesh flecked bubbles massive in streams & foliage adorned skies.

It was the least I might do as an American progeny - *made sense* - to follow as a scion to the single superpower in the world locked in mortal competition with the godless Soviets.

Christ! I have to wear ballistic bulletproof wrap around shades of shame to hide, even to write the recall ...

In the still snow April, our nine sheep would miraculously become twenty-five in a matter of days as birthing occurred in twins and triplets. I fed the wobbly arrivals, watered them, placed tight rubber bands at the juncture of body and dangling furry tail base for farm hygiene.

Long tails gather feces and disease.

When the appendage atrophied and fell away painlessly, I would swab the anus with blue antiseptic. Away they pranced until slaughter.

On a good day on my father's farm, the flock of sheep near, I approached the resident ram. Impulsively, I got down on all fours and began to paw the ground before him. He moved forward head lowered. I thrust my forehead toward him, until the crowns of our skulls met.

Slowly we both applied force. Wavering back and forth, to and fro, we pressed each other. It was really no contest, I could always win if I wished. I chose to beat him only once.

He was so despondent, so utterly depressed in defeat, his relationship to each of the herd altered, wavering. I always let him win thereafter. I couldn't destroy his very kingdom, his crown.

Be simultaneously kind and tender, murderous and boy dictator benevolent.

(That would seem a template for sex and love.)

Preserve fuzzy one's honor, stroke your fingers through their oiled fleece coats in wonder, love and affection – just prior to sending them to death, to sitting down to angelically delicious rack of lamb.

Kill the pet. Kill the innocence – choosing culinary euphoria.

No one was vegetarian, except Hitler, look what that got him. PLANT BASED DIET!! - clear predisposition to blitzkrieg invasions halitosis, genocide, skip dancing in circus 'band geek uniforms' and snorting speed, to cover sexual 'hanging with murderous queens' 'ambiguity' - wilted tiny dick impotence - as Eva Braun gave blow jobs to the bodyguards beneath the Berchtesgaden deck. This guy was so bad in bed girls shot themselves to escape mentorship.

Now, now, I know I'm offending my veg Sistas and Bros – we who are about to alkaline detox doff our bonnets to you!

I merely say we, the Kilpatrick brood were American cowboy postwar seedlings, Normandy and Nagasaki victor children - steak as prize for the winning, grill it once the coals have settled from firebombing Tokyo. Boomtown nation!

Meat – blood medicine to the baby warrior soul - carnivore. I have O+ blood type – one of the newest bloods in the world, perhaps requiring, thriving on fresh kill.

What's good for the goose is good for the gander or as my onetime black (dark chocolate) lover would paraphrase 'What's good for the gander is good for the ducks'. She was the wife of the head CNN entertainment reporter (and the best assistant I ever had, groomed as she was by helping hubby at headquarters in Atlanta and LA) before their dissolving union became violent, cops called, and her taking sanctuary in my home.

She regaled me with incidences of the entire network lying to world audiences, including story white washes, major event blackouts and bold propaganda mutations. And she was given to my opalescent ejaculate being sprayed over her freshly augmented stupendous breasts – her 'visuals' as she called the spectacle between repetitive ghetto racial and man rage. She didn't handle the stress of divorce well.

She was game for anything though and a creature of high humor. As my Jewish Iranian (the Jew from the Axis of Evil) director of photography filmed us' making love'

53

together in a speculative Borat-like piece of appalling non PC graphic rear mounting in which I crooned historical plantation songs in reenactment of Thomas Jefferson and Sally Hemmings – this was pre-breast enlargement, the 'bee sting' mammary period, before she would at my request slip from her top and submerge her moon size neo turbo charged after-market tits in the frosting of a friend's 18-year old grandson's birthday party cake at Brenda's Cigar lounge. On that very night I exhorted fine actor buddy Marty Cove (KARATE KID) to please go out with her, gain pussy access to take the heat off me (which he did) ... by then I had met Mia and was off into true love's ignition.

Marty by the way loves to show up in pajamas at Television Academy events with a huge scarf about his neck. He is deep in that sartorial stage when superb actors - Brando, Burt Reynolds, Cove – flit about in gaudy flamboyance hiding the chicken neck????

<u>Get back on track tangential motherfucker</u> ... if I will eat other beings as I have from earliest age then coming from egalitarian Connecticut, to be on the side of fairness and justice, "What's good for the gander is good for the ducks" I advocate 'self-cannibalism' - everything intrinsically right with my being gnawed upon once dead if I embrace consuming animals. Eat me if you can catch me.

Which by the way, isn't the same as murdering someone for canapes – which is what we do for animals – on a mass scale, organic or not.

I've eaten nothing but organic carcasses, pure provisions,
for my whole life because of mother and father's providing,
and because I care about animals - how each is raised and
lives until kill kitchen kill ... ALONG WITH DEVOTION
TO PURITY. What are they fed? You have to pose such
questions - especially in the case of wild pigs. They'll eat a
rubber Euclid tire while drinking the gut shot hemoglobin
of their own nuclear family.

I might taste passable in earthquake preparedness salt
cured sinew chewy charcuterie. Or merely serve for
'acquired taste' flavor in a post-apocalyptic bone broth.

More likely, warning, by the time I'm done with this
shamble mortal coil you won't get a serviceable scoop of
SOYLENT GREEN to munch on. Go ahead, try the Salt &
Straw sugar cone with heaped Patrick rangy tartare. Put
some fucking berry sprinkles on it!

Is it weird that we sup on creatures – absolutely – AND
YES, I CRAVE A T-BONE AND REVEL IN THE ETHICS
OF HUNTING AND FISHING MY OWN FEAST.

From a pup's age, I illogically existed in this cognitive
dissonance – the grand amour for stalk and kill as well as
immense melancholy empathy for the killed.

I had a fistfight with a close friend when he murdered a
baby robin I had been nurturing in the barn. He used a

snow shovel when the small thing fell from the nest, its mother swooping about in futile protection.

I was outraged at his 'senseless' killing – and yet, wandering for years – even now - in a trail of my own enjoyed, yes even cherished butchery.

I traversed the parents' property with a .22 bolt-action (lethal to a mile) single shot killing. Mice and intricately striped chipmunks in the spring house protecting our water well fell victim - shooting off the pad lock, flinging open the door, blazing seasonal light blinding diminutive creatures, toy yellow flecked hazel eyes bolt on me, holding each of us fast as I executed them one after another.

Bullets passed through their bodies punching light holes in the back plank wall.

Each would slip off the slim stud board they clung to, fall, splash into the sapphire pure liquid below.

The farmers downstream complained of small bloated carcasses, tainting their drinking and livestock waters.

I rescued a male mallard after he was struck by a car, nursed him back with eyedropper milk and bread masticated in my mouth. I stroked his viridian crown and rainbow color feathers, whispering admiration and love, then blew others from the sky by hundreds.

Defend the one, massacre the many. I am an American boy. I am a young male human.

I was looming as a slaughterer, liquidator, atavistically indulging in my inner hunter gatherer. I was imbued too, saved too, simply by the self-delusional concept of simultaneous white knight stories, Teddy Roosevelt split personality. Humanness …

A fat stray cat hassled our kittens. I took him out into the woods and blew his abdomen into gore, not even attempting to pretend I was protecting our felines. I knew everything I was unleashing … purity and murder, cruelty and forbidden ground.

Racing images of childhood –

Playing with sister Kathy in a Bloomfield building site …

Mom beatings for poor grades …

The hulking adult neighbor next door exposing himself like a perverted Robert Duval 'Boo Radley' in TO KILL A MOCKING BIRD …

Older Donny Moore jerking off lying down in our crafted miniature whiffle ball baseball stadium dugout, prick massive, ejaculate Vesuvius Soft Serve, we younger ones watched – *it looked painful* - then scurried away wordlessly, thinking only 'Okay what's next?' …

Sledding behind burly Mr. Dooley – 1st teacher to give a shit and provide male stability, dragging clutching

57

squealing kids throughout the snowy recess on the Bakersville ice-covered school playground …

A fellow girl student's first breasts (Sandra Gahaghan) …

Mrs. Fitzsimmons lashing us (me) often with a yard stick ruler to the head, face and knuckles …

Principal Lovely ordering me to take down my trousers in the boys' room so I could be belted for transgression …

Imagine such 'pedophilic abusive images' in today's elementary institutions. Then it was just 'school'. Lovely was doing what he thought best for the child, *a good, gentle man trying to stem the tide of delinquency with explicit warning of corporal punishment.*

*****

My mother cooked like an American Dream – field fresh salads brimmed full of color, tawny cream puff desserts crowned with her fudge, gorge filled with homemade vanilla ice cream … scratch beef & turkey meatloaf, handmade spaghetti & lasagna, macaroni & newly created cheese, yard grill broiled & stove top pan fried & oven baked chickens, mustard, lingonberry, date bathed savory fish - to this day without parallel in my taste.

Meringues & German chocolate cake, pecan & pumpkin pies, buttered baked potatoes & Maine lobsters, clams, shrimp, ham vinegar infused okra & collard greens, picked moment before corn on the cob, pickled & vined

cucumbers, tomatoes, zucchini & squash, homemade
potpies and black-eyed peas.

Royalty dining perks from the madwoman of Chaillot. Why
should she not be loony? No massages, chiropractic, yoga
or meditation, no juice fasts or wheat grass immunity shots
with a slice of apple on top of the glass, no facials or time
alone, no pharmaceutical intervention for her.

Surrounded by five riotous children, ninja whipped into
poor girl boil heading somewhere, away from the tiny
Floyd Avenue Richmond brownstone she was reared in,
back to the mythical Bethlehem Star plantation, some 20th
century Monticello vison state in the mind – all together in
a crap shoot Silver Pewter Cup kissed for luck by racism,
exclusivity and puritan work ethic. Is it any wonder she
was borderline psycho, brittle bipolar hysterical every
moment issuing such attempted perfection output?

I'm blessed! I always had an interest in rejuvenation and
the sense to seek 'luxury' indispensable tools, *vital as
brushing your teeth* - healing modalities to stave off pain
and madness … were it not for personal athletic power and
bravery, warrior and healer sensibilities … I might easily
have become a broken, perpetual roadrager, imprisoned,
self-medicating – Margot Kidder, Martin Lawrence, Russel
Crowe in the cups, Sean Penn in powder land, Mel Gibson
on a Malibu Road. I know what feeling good feels like, I
know my center and when the balance beam has been lost.

So many do not.

*****

We were given U.S. Pony Club and the children of wealth, equestrian teachers and trained mounts on lead lines, trailers and journeys to hill and dale, moneyed WASP costumed fox hunting exclusivity … the meandering trail of points to valor at Madison Square Garden's National Horse Show.

Mom's ranting for lack of help, flailing in exhaustion, control and hysteria - while perversely refusing aid or any intrusion in the kitchen, anywhere, hurling insults … then off I would go to curry manes and tails, whisper love and reverence, muck the stalls.

We children giggled when Faye slowly poured an entire gallon of milk over my head and flung the container to the floor after I spilled a partial glass on the *garden of deliciousness* table. This was jovial communal humiliation intimacy, so preferable to assault, a kind of love, a light somewhere …

*****

Despite the feasts, I was always hungry as young growing lions are. I learned to clandestine cook and clean up deep in the night, silently, covertly, without wafting odor or residual tells.

I achieved parental benediction, received praise by cleaning up family sit down feeds, dish washing after meals in the kitchen. This allowed me to gobble leftovers. I did this long into adulthood - volunteering at dinner party draw downs, busing, savoring and thieving like Blackbeard boosting baubles on a rolling ship's deck.

Sometimes the hostess having been betrayed by her husband would leave her mate at the table and join me - we'd fuck against the stove or kitchen counter, our liquids anointing the floor in best Anais Nin.

"There are no leftovers with Pat," Mom would say. *Food nor disenchanted wives.*

My sister did the same without my sports fury, attained and remained 250lbs, from pretty child to Dickensian John Candy expanse – always with wit and accomplishment. The nurture/conflict circus kitchen and its became her place of cultivating peace.

It took time and I accepted her as ever beautiful - still the tragedy of those who cannot transform, cannot place themselves, *their own bodies first*, disconnected from the physical when the means is there for all.

They call even mention of such divorce from the physical 'body shaming' now, to validate collective and individual lack of will. Yes, we need to love in all cases, but self-accountability, attempt at personal balance is vital.

Mom was institutionalized several times for 'nervous exhaustion', racing screaming up and down the stairs in pitched hysteria and cursing tears, always refusing medication or treatment.

When she 'went away to rest' father made me simple burnt bacon and fried eggs, his only dish. It tasted *so good,* better than all the gourmet extravaganzas she conceived because he and I were momentarily together, alone and safe.

The house was still for those breakfasts, weather, sunlight and distant trees vivid, war somewhere else.

As we ate I imagined my father with a lean, racy tall blond woman who doted on us, made him happy. He deserved that but somehow, he ascribed some portion of his monumental success to my mother, though this of course is absurd knowing his pre-betrothal track record.

Across the small oval table, father told me we had to excuse her behavior because she was ill. It was, "Up to you son to accommodate her", he said, which didn't sit right for a thirteen-year old son of liberty and revolt.

Even I, tender age, had learned the lesson of non-appeasement of international fart bag bullies (Tojo, Mussolini, Hitler and Stalin) murdering and streaking unhinged through existential morass.

From every source available to a boy or girl:

Newsreel accounts, seminal TV shows COMBAT and THE UNTOUCHABLES with Robert Stack – sanitized conflagration made squad intimate by Vic Morrow and criminal gangland Thompson machine gunning justice in the streets of Walter Winchell narrated Chicago.

You stand up to evil!

Divorce the witch, Have some courage! Protect me, us, and yourself!!!!!! Bastard aggressor Axis bullies showed us the way to respond!

From Churchill and FDR speeches, from TWENTITH CENTURY and Sir Lawrence Olivier's WORLD AT WAR narrations, broadcast documentaries of the time stirring to the young mind!

FROM YOUR OWN GOD DAMN TABLE STORIES OF global conflict round the brawling, epicurean family feeds!!!!!!!!

Evil cannot be appeased.

This was perhaps the very genesis of my world view – tyrants cannot be coddled – much later to become my first, most primal exception and revulsion to Obama ... his apology tour, his trading five Taliban mass murderers for a deserter, his aiding and abetting of Iran with 150 billion and a spineless nuclear treaty.

Why then on a personal level is Mom enabled & sheltered in madness by my godlike Father at every juncture of my childhood - a man who has spent his entire young manhood battling history's greatest barbarities in Europe & the Pacific.

All our minds – every member of the growing family - 3 sisters & a brother mushrooming in this nutrient rich dysfunctional soil - mutate under lack of protection & void of emotional nurturing.

*****

To escape, starting at nine, I stole my parents' tractors and cars. One day as I brought my father's VW 'Bug' back, within sight of the house I saw a small woodchuck trundling the country asphalt.

This is essentially an eastern badger, a New England wolverine. I thought that would be a superb pet. I leapt from the car, grabbed a spare blanket from the forward trunk space, swooped in like a mad magician, cape-enveloped the beast, scooped it up, tied it off and tossed it into the rear seat of the Porsche Fuhrer inspired two door.

Before I could settle in the driver's seat, the dagger clawed, razor toothed animal had shredded the blanket, was tearing the tiny back seat to tatters. In admiring fascination – full knowledge I was in for hellfire for destroying the car - all I could do was open the door, stand aside and let Woodie Chuckie go his way in his own time.

Once Lil' Poo - our cat who lived to 26 years old - proudly brought the severed head of a stalked and eaten woodchuck to the porch doorstep for presentation to us humans.

That is a battle I would have liked to see.

The trophies of the beast and human kingdoms …
murderous duality of man to animals, depraved conquest of
the tame and tiny, domination by large over small, smart
over dim, Darwinian rousting.

My mother seemed as savagely indiscriminate in her
destruction as the woodchuck, with less reason shredding
anything that would lay captive to the soul of her illness.

*****

Language connections grew deeper … this one's eyes were
"like the red veined Dogwood blossoms", that group's
selfish acts "resembled the canopy tent moths in bulbous
sacks supping on trees."

With such authenticate taste buds, gastronomic grooming,
linguistic gifts heading heavenward (humble lol) … cells
reared on true food and elitist, uplifting education; I set out
into my pubescent world.

I was a Life Boy Scout, one merit badge short of Eagle.
('Citizenship in the Home' denied me by my mother. She
refused to sign the certificate. Who can blame her just after
a critter ate the car during my joy ride larceny?). Revenge
politics by a punitive parent … scarring of spit tossed on
hot home side grease.

She became a high school psychologist via prestigious Trinity College, by all accounts vital to her students' very survival and ascension.

When she fixed me up with her favored girl students – "She's cute as a speckled puppy dog!" I made a point of boy steering girl into giving a blowjob on first meeting. They were willing; I was after all Mrs. K's kid. I never spoke to any of them ever again.

I would masturbate before I went out, so supercharged I would cum merely at the touch of fabric, the first female aroma, texture of an ear, if I didn't ease the pressure off the hot James Dean GIANT gusher well prior.

Split in her mind and actions – Faye stopped beside a road tragedy and administered cool first aid to a nearly decapitated man with ease, yet cursed me, then passed out with onrushing blush cheeks, maternal compulsion when I received a small cut.

Lordy, endearingly dramatic even to a wonder boy ...

She tested me, used me as guinea pig to complete her Master's degree course work, and then came up a few hours short of a doctorate and private practice.

Both of us tiny increments from an astounding goal ... by my simple questions, drawing her closer to the witch's brew core of her psychosis, she could be driven always to killing wrath.

This was my ultimate sin: an absorbent inquisitive child arriving with untarnished joy, an intricate instinctual notion of right and wrong, in a space of gale force contradiction, weird cruelty, ruptured, erotically charged human instincts.

This and stealing Christmas cookies from the freezer prior to the actual holiday or reading with a flashlight under blankets after bedtime.

High on adrenaline and asthma speed meds I had to be dragged bawling to bed, so intent that I would not miss anything!

And so, I was flogged body, heart and soul by one parent, left vulnerable, inspired and bewildered by another. Point man on the child patrol, first to trip the parental claymore mine and unleash the ambush.

Not once in my lifetime have I seen my mother kiss or hug any of her children. Not I the eldest, nor my next astoundingly brainy morbidly hefty sister, not my 'gone to the dark side' classically blighted soul next youngest sister, not my brave, stubborn codependent to flawed men youngest sister, not my lifelong addictive, developmentally sweet, criminal and perhaps now, financially astute brain damaged brother, kids of the crucible all grown to men and women.

I am lucky having colorful badges and sash patches of abuse.

I am blessed to be redolent with psyche sorcery: juxtaposition of acts and background abrupt as *inquisition torture amidst renaissance Tuscany.*

Surviving a vigorous reentry – crushed nose, asthma – the earthly karmic battle begins.

By land…

... and sea.

Don't come any closer or I'll give you the spurs ...

Listen, if we dig a hole deep enough, we can bury her here.

Pay attention to an expert Dad, kiss and nibble their ear--
you're home free.

Finest way to avoid maternal butcher knife attacks and beatings with vacuum cleaner cords.

It looks pastoral, 'til they wrap your tail with a blue rubber band so it falls off from lack of blood.

Upside symphony of the manic...

Getting a gallon of milk poured over your head by your Mom is actually an extreme act of intimacy.

After community complaints, the council decided to neuter Patrick. (from left Grandy Pa - mother's father, Uncle Larry, my father Robert at full manhood, hand on my head, Uncle Edwin - mother's baby brother far right, served hard time for pedophilia. Luckily, I was spared.

Mommy please go away for an Advanced Doctorate!

Five: Pivotal Betrayals

"He only lasted six months.
You're one of us now.
We lost a man. A second man!
Did you hear me? A man died." Red One / DARK
ANGEL

John F. Kennedy, wider world King Arthur of my youth, was violently assassinated when I was thirteen.

As a barely pubescent I witnessed vivid 2AM infidelity by mother with my Flash good looking baseball/football coach.

The legend of the goodly and courageous betrayed English mystical monarch & my cuckold father became one as I constructed a life altering infamy of gender/relationship mistrust, preemptive promiscuity & infidelity. My immediate reaction to this seismic loss & hurricane around and within me came in the shape of daredevil escapes – literal and drug induced from home and cops – exuberant, calculated delinquency - and reading *anything, everything,* book a day for years. Literary straight bi-sexual rogues became my heroes.

Cassius Clay, entertaining insurrectionist yell god of my age, became Heavyweight Champion of The World; David defeated guttural Sonny Liston Goliath, an event ripping reactionary elements of the country with rising 'niggrah' sex fear.

I slept in a room isolated structurally from the rest of the Greek Revival home. I awoke uncharacteristically at 2am one night, opening my eyes and ears to stillness in the dark blue.

Propelled by some unseen force, I withdrew blankets from my lean frame and moved through the upstairs.

Houses of the period weren't conceived for stealth, but I was versed in the near balletic exercise of stifling the floor board groans – I had motive and inspiration for this. I was eluding the waking of my mother. Like a stabbed serpent she could rise in an instant to lather bat insanity on idyllic youth and family peace.

This night trip took me laterally to the upstairs room where my three sisters shared the night. Each tucked into their own single bed, dreaming their young lives. I stood still in their room, feeling the moon. I weighed the variable depth and soundness of my sisters' breathing.

Curiosity and early teen imperative sparked off like the concentric rings of an arson gasoline fire flowing through a dry field: what mysteries of form underneath their blankets and nightgowns?

My eyes were pulled to the window. Beyond the waist-high New England stonewall a car was parked. I knew the vehicle, my Scottish Blond 'Immortal Hombre' baseball/football coach's coal black Chevy, pressed near the rock barrier.

Each winter New England stones heave upward from frozen ground and over centuries have been harnessed for land boundaries, pasture containment, domicile protection.

I was in the midst of what I label God's pivots …

I turned from the window and my sisters, made my way back from their room, down the ancient boarded stairs, through the living room, right turn into the dining room, further into the kitchen to the open door to the porch. Quick, unerring, awake yet ethereal.

There on the porch was my mother, her nude beauty against the pillar, mouth agape, silently gasping, strong yet feminine legs clasped around her lover's lower body, his one hand first at her throat, mouth at her breasts, the other hand's fingers tracing rouge white welts on her ass, his cock lancing into her. He raised her one leg higher and the revealing became full. They went on as I stood, a child transfixed, in this act I knew nothing of, only sensed, at the time.

He was married as well. I knew his wife, a lithe blond, pretty woman who wore glasses, a member of my mother and father's circle of adult friends. They came together in 'parties', drinks, pipes for men and Virginia Slims for ladies. Droll activity to me from the windows where I snuck spy smiling glances.

His large hands raked at my mother, and he withdrew, cock pumping, angled …

His froth escaped, she clasped it and I saw cream usher all over her gripped fingers and her thigh, his moaning and shuddering mingling with her head shaking back and fro, auburn hair alternately revealing her features and obscuring her profile. He tilted his face toward the porch roof in agonized religious pleasure.

Her other hand reached upward, found his buzz cut blond skull and drew his mouth to her, out of delirious sensory discord, up on toes, the form of her legs trembling, she directed his lips, each site still rising and falling, breasts, belly clenching …

They pulled apart; she knelt and took his cock in her mouth, the glistening. He held her hand, cupped her head, his face again toward the porch roof from sensation. His fingers traced her lips, feeling the outline of her mouth, tangling in her shoulder length hair.

Her face, lips wet from him, his prick horizontal to the earth … he led her naked and wavering off the porch, down the moonlit stone path, past an opening in the gray/black stone fence. He opened the back door of the vehicle with some chivalry, followed her in.

The door shuts. The night was completely still.

I stood, watched, and listened, hearing nothing but a light laughter, brief ticking of suspension from the car, a kiss of wind in the near maples and birches my father and I walked.

After a moment I turned without judgment, again that incomprehensibility, *a feeling nothingness, merely existing*. I don't remember moving back through the house, but I recall reentering my bed, blankets, immediately asleep.

I awoke in the morning in a world with Kennedy Number One dead in Dallas, brain blown then later betrayed (*in my kid unknowing loyalty to the fine handsome men of my puberty, without knowing of Jack's infidelities, his unleashing of assassinations globally {the Phoenix Program which by estimates murdered 40,000, alongside nine failed Fidel attempts}, his treachery countering the mob, {legally and extra legally}, this protocol disregarding Ivy League arrogant even regularly bored into Sam Giancana's mistress Judith Campbell Exner, his ruthless brother Bobby {kidnapping of organized crime don Carlos Marcello out of Mexico} – both playing Judas to the very killer Teamster Joe Kennedy cronies who placed Jack in power by fraudulent Indiana vote buying. By any 'live by the gun, die by the gun' Buddhist karma scheme the Kennedys were fated to die)* … to my child eyes the only realized crime was by Jackie bolting to a billionaire Greek troll I imagined to be a greasy, dwarfish foul interloper (without realizing her real necessity for security from assassins or perceiving Onassis's charisma).

My father, the finest man I have ever known, sliced by a spun out luscious she, *my Arthur* two-timed by a vitriolic spewing Guinevere and my finest knight B-Ball Lancelot – all of it pulsating through my Sons of the American Revolution 'grip my cock in the shower' consciousness as clearly as the call to rebellion.

How else could I emerge from this amalgam of perceived treachery but with a disruptive counter pull, equal parts allure and deep distrust of goddesses and gods?

Tumultuous hormones, high testosterone Alpha Leo cub, pin pulled on the grenade of my sexuality.

I made it my adolescent art, my lemonade stand, to learn erogenous zones - make it to her ear and you're onto undulating seismic squirming road boy.

I could not, would not, follow my mother's moral leadership ever again. I held the secret for decades, long after confronting my own failures of faithfulness, my lack of fidelity to any woman, however pretty or sweet, mannered or devoted. Perhaps I protected myself by amorous sleight of hand, crossing the boundary before any might drive the stake first into my own flawed, fractured love. I expected betrayal and dealt it, I was entertained by it, accepting of it, longing for loyalty yet always an eye for raw Excalibur to descend splitting the existence of relationship, marriage.

Without moral landing lights, I flew into all manner of behavior, finding my own way by live reckoning, literature and film kings, snatched prayers and some innate sense of battered integrity and one-sided equality, a fierce dedication to individuality, pitted romanticism and shadowy situational responsibility and ethics.

Nothing like watching your smokin' psychotic unbalanced Oedipal she maniac be fucked by the man who exhorts you to greater heights of 'crab soccer' on the polished gym floor for four years ... poster man for leadership, smacking line drive hardballs to you at shortstop on both Junior Varsity and Varsity baseball squads, pumping you warm up pigskin passes to limber the boy for fall gladiator gridiron battles.

I flew psychedelic mushrooms, lost my virginity to a State Trooper's daughter (she was twelve) on a lawn in Norfolk.

At night walking about the small pretty town heaving bricks at corrugated tin buildings & smashing giant plate glass windows of businesses ... just to hear the rattle roar and falling shards shatter.

She had taken a 'course' with the local district attorney's office, 'Parents' Guide to Illicit Child Drug Use,' had absorbed just enough Molotov cocktail atomic info to glean with absolute fanatic jet fueled Aurora Borealis certainty I was 'injecting hash' and 'rolling glue joints.'

Home from drinking and hallucinogenic nights, I tried creeping the stairs to the bedroom but ran into plastic trash bins mother had strewn on the knotted boards. Instantly awake and meth sentry alert, she and I now sitting at opposite ends of the living room in Classical Duncan Phyfe chairs, face to face, our ringside features and eyes dilated fire-in-the sky from different serotonins ... my brain reverberating with LSD, hers with bi-polar righteous investigative powers.

Is it any wonder I never sought 'shamanistic Acid quests', rather preferred risqué edge work at speed when I was chick hatched and reared into Anglo ping-pong shrunken head merry go round?

Seeking oasis from unbalanced parenting (actually oddly balanced - her absolute anger and illogic, his gentle statesman-like love) & *naturally* cultivating teenage exhilarations:

Vehicle, higher and quicker MPH, psychoactive psychotropic misbehavior performance …

My boy drug life married Ducati motorcycles at 152MPH, or downhill suicide Alpine skiing without learning to turn.

I embraced hash oil hysterics, town wide merciless teasing & mimicry, hang gliding peyote flights, biker dervish depth perception distortion – stopping a ½ mile from the red light.

Gulping cereal bowls full of grass/LSD milk to hide contraband from parents resulted in a 3-day trip.

Black ice skidding at high speed, frozen lake racing, blind in snowstorms, dark road power shifting drifting curves away from the law & other boy 'stuff' resulting in repeated hospitalizations.

The classic & meteoric act out of lack of nurturing, rebellion & adolescent caroming about for *any* legitimate code of conduct, seizing one's own moment & era.

Out on the tubular bells filmic penis meteor velocity leading edge rugby scrum was where 'doper and roper' god life lay.

*And so, I read even more - newspaper bits, magazine sheets floating on a stree*t - to escape her seething as she rifled my room, battered into the single bathroom as I defecated, acting like a fuming shivering animal seeking to winterize itself inside before her mental pipes burst from riled frozen ice.

I raced time and history by chapters.

Paperbacks, hard bounds, newspapers, any print, gave me power to span world and space, to free myself from maternal tyranny - achieving singularity, visiting paragons of vice and virtue, love, desire, evil and principles, critical thinking, each and all consumed voraciously.

I remain continually reading, three books, multiple magazines going at a time, volumes, racing time and history by chapters, newspapers … in our age of constant handheld imagery and sound, radio shotgun populism, print and visual sourced opinion and bias.

Literature has given me the instrument of soaring beyond.

My teenage beacons became Fitzgerald, Hemmingway, Kerouac, Cassidy, Kesey and Wolfe, McQuane, Michael Herr, Caputo and Thompson. Literate car thieves and patriotic war knights, mad cultural maniacs, perfections of individualism and momentary pleasure, Lady Killers, hetero cocksucker hotdogs.

Above all they lived, gulping not simply every moment, but each second and all the thin silver and gold filaments of personal existence.

When I was fourteen, Faye went to hit me once more for no reason except wanton incoherence. I shoved her back, she hung suspended, quivering slightly for balance on the 2nd story top step, then tumbled end over end down the stairs. She arose at the bottom, silent berserk creature, adrenaline and fearless psychopathic frenzy in her eyes.

"Don't ever hit me again," I said with surprising, steely quiet. And she never again laid a hand on me.

Six: Invulnerable Child Seeking Balance

"That's why God evented Plan B. Alright earn your keep. Get us out of sight." Trevor Jankowski / BOOMTOWN

I became Golden Athletic Adolescent - star of football, baseball, wrestling, equestrian arts, swimming champion above & below the surface money challenge winner - all this outside an amoral home life cyclone of maternal adultery, racial & religious separatism, crazed minefields of verbal & physical attack - each outburst IED deployed & randomly clicked off by trip wire Faye.

I was never allowed friends in the home. *Not once.* Given the local Connecticut demographics they'd have invariably been Italian and Catholic, *Papists* in my mother's vernacular, foreign species counter to the American Revolution and the Confederacy. She had insidious, percolating fear of intermingling, soiling of the seed, dark swarthy fetuses – worse still social and sex co-dancing with Jews and other interlopers of the line.

Don't beat it to death – gratitude for those things that were superb.

After my mother's IMAX infidelity (and she knew I knew, her anger and guilt more Pompeii suffocating and lethal than ever) my drive outward to girls and women intensified. I spent an inordinate time in the company of my young friends' mothers.

Married, divorced, widowed, I slept with some, excursions over menstrual blood and marital vows, red river of adultery and desire. They offered me money on occasion and always served up psychological warmth. I know I was looking for female haven, a sense of home port missing from my theater of parental combat, all of it with wide-eyed teenage spellbound sex cravings. Boys being boys, girls being girls …

At home, my mother like embryonic Soviet rocketry achieved firestorm initial lift, then reared back earthward, detonating in fireball, gas and ash, quick frying all those arrogant and dumb enough to set up lawn chairs to watch the launch …

… akin to being a naive military minion placed a half-mile from early atomic blasts (as my father was) "Here son, don these dime store Ray Bans when the mushroom cloud engulfs you. If you feel your genitals crisp up or your eyeballs give off vaporizing cornea wisps that's SOP normal, just don't masturbate in the barrack's shower stalls and we've free lobotomies for one and all courtesy of the CIA."

Hey Niggah, come 'on ova here and let's castrate ya just a little … its fer governmental explorating and medical advanment …

I took on THE SISTERS, two fetching multi-lingual mothers of friends – actually they took me under wing, carrying me to a Fellini-like ménage a trois with them.

*Musing on recent accusations of sexual assault against
Asia Argento by a 17-year old young man. How insipid
this 'troubled male' creature must be to seek $380,000
from Argento and Anthony Bourdain when mass segments
of the global teenage male population would give a left
testicle to have it on with a tattooed Italianate performer.
Yes, its preferable to diminish the Left semen.*

*God rest Tony's soul, has anyone investigated the
possibility that the 'Parts Unknown' host offed himself due
to CNN bias, Trump derangement and the repeat affair
with troll Weinstein?*

On my occasion, as I was being 'statutory raped'- *one
cannot harass the willing* - the affair was cooked up and
made tasty facile by the English-speaking sister of the
MILF, who spoke only Spanish and German.

There was a fierce antagonism toward the husband, an
American diplomat posted to Germany and back, both
sisters wishing to bring pussy prick retribution upon my
friend's father.

The elder, darker sister translated the seduction, verbally
subtitling our actual fuck utterances. As I rose and fell, the
married woman beneath me, her legs entangling my 13-
year-old hips, her sister's face was always nearby,
coaxing, urging, speaking both Spanish and English,
occasionally German. I would be lying if I said this was
anything but beyond arousing - I felt myself luckiest of
boys.

They offered me $3,000 dollars – a large sum at the time –
plus room and board, to accompany them back to the
husband's post in Germany for a year. My 'cover' as her

son's friend was ideal, I became an exchange amigo secret agent with penis security clearance. OO *license to ...*

I was enthusiastic for the adventure, splitting home my fondest aspiration – so much so I wrote the following:

"Leaving, passing away from the patina of passions, free from erupting shells and cries of wounded siblings, escape, heart minerals pristine in car and air, hails of solace in the scream of rubber ..."

The voyage to Germany went 'poof' one day, while our trio of sex conspirators was submerged in trilingual sex, my boyish tool wiling away in the wife, sister whispering ... "Your body, I'm raping you, your husband watches as I pierce you!"

(A floret phrase I have sporadically reissued.)

The husband, suspicious, had hired a duo of rough necks – minor sub mafia in the small Connecticut town, omnipresent foot thugs in every New England berg.

The pair burst into the room, went for me. I had already shot from the bed, catching my ankle in a sheet, sisters screaming and cursing in tongues. I fell, seperating my shoulder, leapt out the window, nude, never seeing the women again.

Had I stayed -

Ground into blutwurst at the direction of the cuckold husband, or Italian meatball salsiccia or perhaps polpette Italiane by the thugs doing the grinding?

I imagine the conversation in their bedroom summit after my exit.

The two on two situation ... primary colored tailored feminine wardrobe splashed about ... a black haired white fleshed woman naked, mouth wide in interrupted startling spasm ... close by her tempestuous red headed ring master sister ... a pair of opportunistic laborer neo killers hot and foiled in their mission, backs, thighs and groins straining at cheap Sears fabric ...

I imagine each able to swivel their appealing treachery discourse and sexual currents to each other, propelling one another into sultry, unsheathed chit chat ...

You, you, and you ... oh, you're fine ... bella donne ... pene enorme ...

Yeah ...

My bello cretino ... my open conchiglia ... yes on top of me magnificent massive man ... I stroke your sides and thighs.

Yeah ...

Ich will deinen harten Schwanz in meiner fotze fuehlen...
We want your hard cocks in our perfumed slits ...

Yeah mam ...

di seta duro pene
His cock is hard silky.

Yeah ...

Fill me with cream valentine glaze…my husband ignores
me when I cry …

Sie haben uns die Liebe sowohl uns zusammen machen,
fangen meine Muschi

You have us, make love to both of us together, and capture
our bodies …

To my injured and streaking escape – another of my
friends, in divine kismet ripped by in the go-cart we had
crafted, capable of 125mph (adjusted to the fact the frame
sat less than one inch from the ground) and so jet engine
loud, criminally infamous and grossly illegal one could
only roll it out from the 'secret' garage location, fire it up
and do one blistering drifting run and U-turn on the block
back to the barn before police would be on their way.

I jammed my slim frame behind him, wrapped my hairless
arms and legs round his body, penis nicely tucked, making
sure no skin was still in contact with the road or blistering
pipes. We were in his house in seconds, me dressing in his
early band t-shirt and corduroy trousers.

A call was placed to my friend's endearing older sister (all
knowing, utterly empathic intelligence with compelling
beauty) eerily unspeaking, she never uttered *one word* in
over a decade as I existed in rapturous crush for her angelic
spirit, her gymnast elaborated calves and torturously full
breasts). Once she arrived she and I were bound for my
home in moments, the princess at the wheel of her yellow
Corvette.

I cradled my injured arm against the road reactive ride, deep in shotgun Recaro racing profile seat, bracing for the verbal and physical onslaught I knew coming from ma mere.

Whenever I came home with a black eye, graphic bruise, a ligament torn from a hip in sport, *rather than sympathy,* each wound in their own way was clear evidence to her of my cross the behavior border bad seed.

When we glided home in clear winter air so pure it seemed to cause life, like the sea of the Caribbean, the full splendor of snow and trees over fields ... the presence of this long graduated gymnastic team captain - a shiny bauble testament to my mother's past coaching - diverted the tantrum.

Mother went straight to her medical rescue mode rather than deranged beast insanity.

How good she and my father were in this - the parental cavalry galloping to eradicate life or limb menacing episodes.

... motorcycle calamities, white bones stabbing outward from compound fractures ... overnight appendix rupture with systemic poisoning ... tonsils, stiches, smashed nose, fishing hooks through feet, tennis balls cutting retina. They were always there to the quick with money and resources.

They did the same for my baby brother to the tune of one million dollars in fees for eleven different rehab institutions and legal fees.

He was always criminal dancing to raise ready bucks to feed the furnace of addiction … theft of Porsches to elaborate kidnap extortion plots in which he was victim to be ransomed. Academy Award winning drug addict histrionics in the short term …

Less than a mastermind, David was quickly revealed in this cute stuff - resulting in multi-state federal court cases, local cops, warrants and incarcerations – my parents were there for him with lawyers and treatments as much as they were for me whenever I racked up vehicle or body.

David had his own need for speed. I once rolled up to him as he changed all four tires on a Jeep.

"What happened?"

"Flipped it, blew out all of 'em."

Contemplate how much air you have to pull to do a complete airborne loop in a jeep and land unscathed with such force you rupture every tire.

Mother and father did precision loops for me whenever I was damaged – I gave them ample bloody opportunities - calling up top surgery talent and hospitalization teams.

My father's increasing executive power, my mother's phys-ed acumen, their dual statewide cultural presence, instrumental in the ability to curry the best medical pros.

While in hospitals I swooned with perfumed temptress nurses. Nurses have been kind to me, particularly girl Candy Stripers (unfortunately now they wear ill-fitting blue or green scrubs). Then they moved about in crisp mid-calf skirts, living teenage Christmas treats, no clear medical purpose except patient resurrection via wholesome teenage breeding eagerness.

Mae West purred, "Nothing to do, and a lotta time to do it."

Later at a quite different end of the caregiver spectrum as an actor, one night I was ably treated by gargantuan emergency room cross-dressing nurses (*a whole tribe*) – the transsexual medical staff at a San Fernando Valley Hospital at 3am when I slashed my fist washing dishes while tripping on psilocybin in a warehouse.

At the time I was separated from my wife, a sabbatical if you will, living in a cavernous warehouse in North Hollywood and marathon fucking actresses in a parked solar powered Airstream trailer.

The restored Airstream was the sole possession I had taken from the marriage. Slapped it on the Toyota Land Cruiser and rolled away.

It was stifling, suffocating in the hangar – the only place I could find in LA large enough to park the fucker.

I achieved both literal and emotional bleed off by tottering to and fro in the vast corrugated space, gripping a fifth of artisanal vodka, my lonely animal heart bellowing – the acoustics were great - happily and simultaneously mournfully.

It passed the time between red headed white skinned jezebels in Lt. Edition Corvettes and the acting gigs as villains.

And so I sliced up my fingers being a tidy hallucinating inebriate.

I have no idea why this particular Los Angeles Valley hospital chose to transform itself into a burlesque nexus of amputated cocks and exaggerated Adams apples, size 15 infirmary sandals and erratic five o'clock shadow facial electrolysis.

Simply desire on the part of humans to gather and stomp together in gaggles?

I received stitches in my hand and bravura Frankenstein flirting from seven-foot tall Amazonians made startling and grotesque by my abrupt, wavering hallucinogenic veers.

*****

I was always in saving peak shape for my teenage debacles, Red Cross Life Guard – football, baseball, basketball, high and wild atop horses, fencing, collegiate wrestling, boxing, rugby … I offered up a muscle ready resilient target.

After the boudoir fall the winning preeminent orthopedic doc gave me a choice - limited arm mobility with an unsightly lump or surgery with a slicing scar from mid chest to scapula. Surgery would also mean a week's stay in hospital and then later, continuing ability to heave long quick throw outs from shortstop.

I had years of Little League and Babe Ruth baseball, I was captain, on my way to Yankee Stadium celebrating the international youth competition - silver dollars and ice cream cones for homers.

I chose the operation and week vacation.

Within three weeks, I was doing pushups, communing with my mothers, stabilizing wires freakishly exiting my back. I have always had a way of surviving swiftly - wheel chair tricks in a full body cast, filming with jagged stitches and a broken nose.

*****

I did have a true surrogate mom at this time - at last finding poignant 'safe harbor' with my best friend Craig's family.

While Shirley's town wrecking boozing pro-fighter husband horrified us, she saw fit to make her home my oasis, fielding my mother's warpath calls, offering winking cover, serving up shared working-class meals and a cheeky heart to the antics of her son and me.

Always a smile and her own loving endurance, it couldn't have been easy with her violent spouse looming.

Storied Dick would corner his son and me, towering over us, a poisoned T-Rex of a man.

The pater monster would stab a hard, thick Irish American index finger into our solar plexus, backing us against the wall, his scabbed knotted knuckles barring retreat. Crown Royal or 7&7 breath fumes noxious and hot cascaded our faces. His mean speech was garbled and incomprehensible, always carrying some morality parable.

Cops came to the home and bars to arrest him, his Krakatoa insurrections quickly painted into local legend. Billy club beatings, splintered furniture and glass, broken teeth, jaws and eye sockets order of the day.

Shirley, her young pretty daughter Sandy, my buddy Craig all endured this embarrassment and pain (public in a river town called Winsted) until Big Dick saw the light and went sober, channeling his rehab and redemption into daily bicycle circling of the local lake, season after year 'til he died near ninety.

They loved Dick and he them.

All of us of the town - Godenzi, Seaback, Serafini boys and girls, Reidys, Moraskis and Joneses - countless more, had their communal dysfunctions, nocturnal hells and homeland agonies, in turn weeping and crushed, always fierce and jovial. We all became not only battered children but exultant merciless humorists in the mill city spilling over with natural beauty.

In my memory which one means more to me? The protectors and guardians, the mimics or sexualized angels, intimidators and tyrants? They all mean something of love for me.

Many are dead. Drugs, Viet Nam, bulimic Auschwitz-like self-starvation, carbon monoxide inhalation, run over in parking lots, caged in prison or institutions … others in assisted living, separating body and mind from mortal place, alternatingly sharp, witty, then dimming, repeating tiny questions and observations over and again.

I can only say they were all perfect, Monet reflected in the waters of lakes.

Seven: Shipped Away, Scholastic Failure and Desire in Dixie

"What He Lacks Is a Good Set of Tits." Denny Kessler/ NIP/TUCK

I was, with my parents' best intentions, exiled/returned to sender to the very same prestigious Virginia boys' prep school – Woodberry Forest - where my father had been a math teacher when I was born years before.

I am fortunate and grateful for their devotion to education.

So, it was off to upper echelon Woodberry for me – American Revolution & Confederate veined class & racial segregation, blacks restricted to the balcony of the local theater - BYE BY BIRDIE flickering on the screen one weekend and Elvis Presley's ROUSTABOUT next. 'Lil Princeton of the South' it was called, the same orange/black tiger mascot, rigorous study as the Ivy League university in Trenton, New Jersey.

Yankee Boy plummets to strange, hostile hormone mad South cub club, wealth & lack of females with 300 wildcats.

*****

I had even by this tender age soundly rejected the Confederacy for its flawed cause and failure to answer cries of universal freedom … despite simultaneous immense pride in being a Virginian American patriot boy. The few Confederate flag wavers at Woodberry were the same precocious entitlement brats who ridiculed my New

England home. I've been eligible to join the Sons of the Confederacy since birth, and since earliest conscious memory shucked the notion of joining an enclave of racial bondage rationalization - even while being stirred by generals and captains, lieutenants, privates, ensigns and sergeants, mistresses, wives, spies, Underground Railroad runners, 65,000 Black soldiers (15,000 who fought in mortal combat) wearing the Rebel Grey – honorable & bold men and women – on both sides of the cruel Civil War. This embodied no cognitive dissonance for me, no disruption of "All men are created equal," "We hold these truths to be self-evident."

Of course, Thomas Jefferson becomes eternally more perplexing, the stunning poet of our revolution, a political visionary the likes the earth has never before seen, whose astounding precepts are even yet to be fully realized, Carnally and certainly romantically with Sally Hemmings, living a reality that was clearly false and hideous – even in his time - that black people were either sub human children or beasts unable to govern themselves and live in freedom. And further, introducing anti-slavery legislation 27 times in his political career – all defeated - still, unable to free his slaves even at his own death, unlike other great Virginia families who willingly gave slaves freedom.

Jefferson in the end valued his wine cellar over the very core of his liberty being, fearing plantation bankruptcy and slackened tipsy leisure over loss of his literate soul.

His is a flaw as disturbing as the idea of original sin. TJ is perhaps the apex example illustrating the Hindi precept that man/woman is incapable of perfection. Each woven rug must by necessity contain a deliberate flaw of craftsmanship – mistakes intentionally placed in order to acknowledge contradiction.

What lesson? We are Jeffersonian in the final analysis, but not him. We must not become him but take his brilliant words and manifest them fully.

Can we have evolution of spirit if statues of these figures are destroyed, even moved elsewhere? Even in genocidal anger by people of color, even in righteous alignment of wrongs and waves of emboldened cultural and ethnic identity?

*****

300 is a renowned Spartan Frank Miller inspired film now but in my dawn of puberty it was simply the number of fevered boys thrust together in a same sex, no sex cauldron of scholastic and athletic flourishing, deprived and stimulated just as their bodies and minds cried out for female contact.

We all burned for the local girls, glimpsed on brief parole Saturday afternoon, the few hours we were time released from the academic prison.

The local town was so insular and inbred when we played the high school baseball team, every member - all nine on the field and each on the bench - was named either Clatterbuck or Clatterball.

I groped my first roommate's penis while he slept and then terrified I might be caught, preemptively, indignantly reported he had inappropriately touched me.

Boldly calculating little 'bearing false witness" liar I was, possessing innate criminal cunning.

The school simply reassigned me to room with the son of the doctor who had, perhaps inebriated, delivered me.

Perfect funnel finishing school for southern manhood …

We were one and all haunted by a single suggestive female … one woman who certainly celebrated her pulse gun effect on the 300 jacked young scholars. The wife of the athletic director, himself a Scots descended demigod figure, this woman moved about the halls, breasts impossibly high and full, legs visions of temptation, condensing about her knowing, enigmatic smile. She strode a path in the perfection of her sex power and made us weak with want.

Each night at 10 pm lights out, I would coerce the doctor's son into telling me fabricated fairy tales of sexual misadventure with her while I stroked myself to culmination. Laughably he struggled against my mental manipulation to no avail.

There is something deeply amusing in a person who is utterly appalled at the depraved nature of your imagination and coercion – yet still carries out your seemingly bizarre wishes.

Actually, there is absolute method to this madness that serves filmmaking, drama itself.

Comedy and deep friendship, extraordinary media creation, a successful empowered and communicative love affair or marriage, all come from the shared ability to say and do almost anything – without borders - with mutual acceptance and trust.

Get the fucking footage, it's always superb! Get the goddamn image, get your cock in your lover and take the high ground.

Sort out the embarrassment and the perceived lack of dignity later. Art comes from the courageous. Nothing is more sinful than boredom!

And besides it's fun!

And guess what, it's those very same inclinations that generate the very images that cause film to be pivotal and make actors famous and endearingly loved by audiences.

Here are some samples that initially would result in set chaos and repulsion … lol …

Nude long-distance sniper shooting, both spotter and triggerman naked and pressed tight against each other as Marine Recon consultants and teachers look on aghast …

Forcing a young masculine actor to wade the roaring Montana Missouri River in his birthday suit … the foaming rapids lapping at his cock …

Tying a nude performer to a stake and shooting (boom sparking arrayed explosive targets surrounding them ...

Causing an actor clad only in an elaborate ornate mask to cavort behind the high flames of a fire pit surrounded by wild boar, the vividly colored skyward heat and sparks obscuring his naughty parts ...

How I love them for doing this even as they mentally revolt and tremble, faces twisting in momentary dismay and revulsion. *Here's the final reality - we never even ultimately revealed any genitals. That's not what it's about - who wants an X rating! No one! What idiot would willingly diminish their audience? Certainly not me?*

<u>*It's not about pornographic exposure, it's about the shot (still or video), the footage!*</u>

I love actors and actresses who will deliver the goods so a preeminent photographer or cinematographer can capture the fission. I have always calculatingly risked a great deal in my own career for the right shot, I would never ask an actor to do anything I wouldn't do – physically or mentally.

An example – we did a movie pitch based on the 1937 Rape of Nanking, a largely unknown genocide carried out by the butchering Japanese in China. 600,000 slaughtered, 120,000 Chinese women raped. But fabulous story, female centric, great emotional and betterment of mankind power amidst unimaginable horror! How do you face terror so unspeakable yet not resorting to violence?

How do you create a poster, a single image that conveys that tragedy of legions of women raped, humans butchered and yet doesn't turn people off, instead drives people to want to see a movie?

I took an Asian American woman friend – Maya Sakura - very beautiful, had her lie down in a Christ crucified pose on a white floor naked, then draped a blood red sash over her breasts and vagina (symbol of the Japanese conquest) and had Ron Jaffe – one of entertainment's most prolific lensman – shoot her downward from atop a step ladder.

Not one pornographic thing – <u>but Maya had to get into position naked to make the shot work.</u>

I had dear actress friends turn the job down. What did that achieve? They took themselves out of being the center of an completely discreet extraordinarily powerful image – art.

It helped that I met Maya when she was completely nude at the PLAYBOY mansion. She was working, and her raw body was painted fully in some advertising campaign.

Be bold warriors! Protect yourselves colleagues but don't abdicate your courage in creation!

At Woodberry, all 300 of us boy students were a metaphor for the world desperate for relief and release …
imagination and delusion, one and the same, each of us prancing, leaping, burst sprinting toward a personal dream world.

A remarkable, high bar institution, I failed three out of five subjects – walking with confusion and vague loneliness, under and within the canopy of the chosen.

Hardly the poorest student but light years away from the wealthiest, I was cast as an outsider Yankee in the Confederacy, and adversely a strange Rebel when home in the summer North.

I won ten dollars one night on a first bet as Cassius Clay soared over Sonny Liston, a tiny triumph in a severe year.

I found an early finesse as a 127lb wrestler coached by a hunchback dwarf. Believe me, it is very difficult to pin a hunchback dwarf.

I attended daily Episcopalian chapel, fell asleep in Bible study (which I regret, wishing I could now instantly summon the majesty of the ancient literature.).

The Drifters ("Under the Boardwalk", "Up on the Roof") played our prep school prom. *That's sweet air buddy – the fucking Drifters for a teen hop!* A lovely chaste girl, made the trip from Connecticut with her parents to be my date.

After she left I hooked up with a drifting female for some sex on the polished floor of the gym – echoes of young lust in the same cavernous varnished smooth cool space where we wrestlers intentionally held our breath until we passed out … early attempts at transcendent exploration.

Isn't it intriguing that wanderers, lovers, sex fiends and high seekers find each other?

I felt the kindness of one or two real young leaders, a
Prefect named Fitzgerald offered an older brother presence.

A most memorable moment for me came as I was shuffling
the brick paths to yet another interminable study hall. I
found myself on Nov. 22, 1963 suddenly beside
Headmaster A. Baker Duncan, 6'9 dead ringer for Abe
Lincoln.

"How are you son?"

"Well Sir, I'm flunking 3 of 5 classes. I got some demerits,
to work them off so I could go to the Episcopal High
wrestling match, the Discipline Board sent me to your
house to garden. Thinking I was cleaning the small pond, I
pulled out the plants. Your koi fish have all suffocated ...
(a long beat) and they just murdered John F. Kennedy".

We ambled mute for a distance. Then from his great height
he turned to me, placed his hand on my 4'11' shoulder.

"We'll be alright".

Together we walked on.

*****

I had a first primitive surgery at Woodberry on the nose
that had been shattered and unrepaired by the 'tipsy' doctor
at birth.

In those days nasal surgery was done awake out of fear that
full unconsciousness would cause one to drown in one's
own blood. So, I stared upward, *wide-angle fish eye lens,* a
'surgeon' injected Novocain needles into my tissues, his

scalpel sliced my nostrils, skin flaps flung backward and hard chiseled, cracked hunks of bone were split away.

On my first day back home, I stripped my striped 'Tiger' tie, grey slacks and blue blazer uniform and danced about brazenly nude.

I spun around, making loud wasp-like sounds, banging my bare ass against my sisters' hips. "I'm a bad bee!!!! I'm going to sting everyone!!"

To my mother, having undamaged aspirational furniture was a high priority ... providing emotionally conducive underpinnings for humans not so much. I don't mean to be cruel, merely accurate.

Now, more than half century later, as she nears death herself, she seems to express love – or is it merely the drugs and the desperate vulnerability of the dying consumed with guilt. I'd like to think both our abilities to give love and forgiveness have thankfully expanded.

Exhausted from the naked insect cry for attention, I promptly fell dead asleep, sprawled legs, genitals utterly displayed, on the stain-free couch plastic; (oddly the same winner takes all pose selected for me by a top photographer years later for a mag shoot). This was both a violent act of revolution and insult to the furniture.

I awakened to the screaming of my enraged mother (her default emotion for all) after my sister did an expressive tattle.

Wordlessly, my father took me to the barbershop for a haircut in the late afternoon, and then going home gently explained the masculine necessity not to perform such depravity after a certain age in life.

I was made to sleep in the car and a nearby cabin for several nights for my own safety, banished from the family and my mother's righteous assaultive anguish.

'Bad bee' sent her round the bend. Wild stinger too close to home.

Two local friends came over to sleep in the cabin. We quickly rolled my father's pipe tobacco in notebook paper and glued it together with Elmer's, lit up, got toxic death green and raving drunk on a sloshing mixture I had incrementally stolen from my parent's bar.

A gallon jug of dishwater colored mixology – part Gallo wine, crème de menthe, whiskey and Miller High Life.

Simple adult mirroring, cocktails and smokes ... it definitely made sense at the time.

As we weaved one tiny step away from vomit in walked my father. He lifted me up with his massive hand, my face kissing close to his. I belched drunken derisive laughter at him.

He slapped me *hard*, smashed my newly repaired nose. Blood flung onto my friends, we all instantly sobered. *Then began careening about in inebriated agony and vomiting ...*

He dragged me – my view pitching about, tree tops to isolated staggering feet - back to the main house. At sight of my face … red snot bubbles over smeared death mask, mother launched herself weeping, screaming at my father.

Sweet fuck, are these two confusing?

He didn't mean it, just misgauged his power. (Years later I visited Virginia Beach doing research on a script about the Underwater Demolition Teams. I spoke with father's vet friends. He told me Dad had simply slapped an Army brute in a bar, propelled the bully across the room and through a glass window.) The man had brawn on tap.

I was allowed back in the house on Sunday evening just in time to gather round the three-channel TV with the family. All communally gazing on the black and white glow as 4 Liverpool Mop Tops were introduced by quivering Ed Sullivan, massed swooning girls and then later the lying, sweating blinking visage of Nixon, repugnant and revealing to a 13-year-old.

"I Wanna Hold Your Hand", "I Saw Her Standing There" – into a shimmering bust-the-dam reservoir catalog of James Brown, Four Tops, Otis Redding, Sam Cook, The Buckinghams, Gene Chandler, Gene Pitney (The Rockville Rocket), Jerry and The Pacemakers, Outsiders, The Kinks, Dave Clark Five, Chad and Jeremy, Jan and Dean, the Beach Boys, Young Rascals, Chubby Checker, Everly Brothers, Rolling Stones, Iron Butterfly, Yardbirds, Bryds and The Animals, Humble Pie, John Mayall and the Bluesbreakers, Small Faces, Zeppelin, Cream, Traffic,

Jefferson Airplane, The Doors, Blind Faith, Barry McGuire, Donovan, Zombies, Trogs, Janis, Dylan, McCoys, Moody Blues. Paul Revere & the Raiders …

Rhythms and sway… music and a marauding child.

Returning to the prestigious prep school was happily ruled out of the question because of my recovery from facial battering.

Still, Woodberry has stayed with me all the days of my life. So rigorous was the scholastic trial, I never again had difficulty in any school.

Eight: Devil Boy and a Love for All

"I love the ambiance you've created here. The objets." Bo / PALMERS PICKUP

Summer job in a factory, I made electrical coils, a vital component in so many instruments of the aerospace age. The top-like wire objects were made in one section of a dark and fiery building, pressure coated with plastic resin by massive machines in my section.

There was a challenged man who stoked the mill furnace, keeping the flame at peak ferocity through his entire shift. He was hardly handsome, but I realized he possessed the lean, stark, inbred and sooty visage of heroic mine workers throughout the world, like someone digging out from under heavy bombardment at dusk, or the ravaged face of a merchant marine sailor pulled from oil engorged waters after a German U-Boat attack, a portrait of industrial Soviet grit bathed in sepia light.

You get the idea – his face was dirty, malnourished, surrounded by hellish flame.

We high school snots kept our distance. He possessed little of interest to our unformed sensibilities and limited bully brains. Still he has stayed with me all my life, his white/ red bulging eyes peering from beneath the grime.

Nearby was a spectral spinster, perhaps in her forties. Ida was easily startled, intensely Catholic in a voodoo suspicious way. She had extraordinary trouble grasping our juvenile dementia and humor, crossing herself often in self-protection against the deep distress our antics and very existence called forth.

It was her job to inspect the finished thingimijigs after the coating process, culling for flawed, deformed output. Day after day, we placed racks of fresh coated coils before her. Hour after hour, she reviewed and selected units that would make their way into the space race, the defense department, steel, oil, agriculture, the twister of great industries of America.

One day, being an exuberant young psychopathic ass, I caught a bat in a creep spot deep in the factory, pitifully flapping for freedom against a dim crusted window. I gleefully placed the terrified flitting beastie in the massive steel mold. Heedless of its struggle, I descended the steel trap, pressed the proper buttons and injected scalding tawny resin plastic around the creature, drowning it, freezing the fluttering appendages, mouth and eyes in eternal fear and agony. Encapsulated terror.

"All humans are Nazis when it comes to animals." – Isaac Bashevis Singer. I don't say that to lessen my crimes by spreading the sin.

I ceremoniously placed the brutal ornament on Ida's work bench. For a second she blinking in non-comprehension then the full horror dawned. She screeched in nervous collapse, staggering backward from the horrible talisman, denouncing me as "Devil Boy! Devil Boy!"

We thought it hilarious.

She remained petrified at what I might conjure beyond, and yet, she and the furnace man found each other and fell in love. I realized then there is someone for everyone in the world.

*****

The massive machine I worked on was setup to prevent horrific accidents by a double button system. The one-ton top would ascend automatically when the injection process was done, revealing two finished coated coils, which I would pluck out and place in a neat row within a nearby Ida bound box.

I would then set the two bare electrical embryos in the machine, slide my arms from beneath the one-ton press, reach wide in opposite directions and press two large separated red buttons, causing the huge steel press to only then descend atop the coils, allowing the machine to follow on with hot injected plastic around the interior buried instruments. When the timed coating process was done, a bell rang and the mammoth upper half heaved itself open once again.

Repeat, repeat, repeat, repeat.

One day, one moment, as I stood a foot away breaking for a few seconds, the mammoth top machine came down by itself without me pushing the two separated buttons.

If my arms had been inside I would have lost *both* arms above the elbow, the mashed flat flesh, squashed scarlet

114

bone and sinew within the machine with mottled misshapen plastic.

Life with two stumps, a wandering existence never to feel with fingers, to grasp a football pass, never to touch the face of a child or the neck of a lover – *never to finger fast till the fountain of female ejaculation.*

I stared awed, deeply fearful. I took it as a sign, fled to other part time 'occupations' - dishwasher, truck driver without a license, Sears Roebuck black market counter teenage shoplifter, camp counselor, swimming/rowing/tennis/sailing instructor.

I'm out of here! Devil Boy is *fucking* gone, moving on to other climes.

Nine: Growth and the Angel

"This is a third world situation. The old values don't work here. I bet you're a real live wire." Al Humphries / SOLDIER OF FORTUNE, INC.

At a dance in a 'lodge' by this lake where ice cars and motorcycles with spiked tires raced going back to the early 20th century, drivers suffering amputation, sometimes dying from arterial bleeding when stabbing tires on loosed machines ripped their arms and legs, I made a move to this Italian American schoolmate.

In the view through the huge glassless windows behind her barefoot champion water skiers, my friends among them (one soon to be decapitated in a car wreck) were sending up massive comets of water. The spraying fluids seemed symbolic of my internal reaction to her. She was full-bodied already, black hair a cascade of curls, a child woman.

"Would you like to dance?"

"Boy, are you crazy?" she rigidly cooed, "I'm Joe Maestrobono's girl."

She spoke like it was a dictate of the God's creation, warm, poignant, aware of nuance…this attachment carried some sharp certainties.

Then this terror was coming at me…a goodly portion of the sub mafia delinquent culture, there in my young eleven-year-old face.

Four of them, each seventeen or more, drop outs airborne from school, hardened by ignorance and failed social engineering, untended by team sports and education, nurtured on petty theft and parental neglect.

I ran.

They came on, picked up speed behind. I plunged from the lodge, rock and roll band sounds growing less distinct, crashed into the trees, branches tearing at my cheeks. Fear, to the point of tears, rasping for breath from my open mouth, their laughter and clamoring faded.

And that was the way it was for the next three years.

Whenever I came to a public place, they arrived and I fled blind into running, hiding, finding my way home by dozens of miles, hitch-hiking the night, amidst trees and shadow shapes.

*****

One summer my own miracle occurred. 127lbs puppy to 185lbs of young man, sprouted from a 'miniature tiger' bench sideline dork, more interested in moths and beetles beside the field, to a 'Man Missile' toppling varsity seniors. The transformation was startling, most double take humorous of all to me.

I was given prophetic nicknames - 'Killer', 'Monster' - on the money given future movie roles. Coaches allowed me free run of fields to intercept and destroy as I chose. Perception and precognition of opponents' movements enhanced and flourished, abilities I know surface from our eternal warrior and hunter ancestry. I knew to whom quarterback handoffs were going, where fullbacks were launching to sweep. I could sense a baseball batter would hit to a place simply by watching a single warm-up ritual swing.

Circles, biological physics.

I climbed on top of asthma by sheer perseverance amidst the social skills provided by my parents. With his easy, natural Under Water Demolition Team (UDT) affinity for water (father was a Pisces) and mother's intense aspirations for her children, I was ushered into the lake Red Cross swimming program.

I became a lifeguard. My lungs, expanded by bronchial struggle, allowed me to race underwater beyond others. I earned money - *cash* - challenging and betting marks I could do this … meditating in motion, Zen husbanding breath beneath perfect calm/tumultuous bodies of liquid.

Once I launched off a Boy Scout camp dock in a contest with four other scouts, entire camp on shore, wrestling, cheering and crying out with that nice joy freedom energy … protected childhood self-determination.

By the time I surfaced, the others had emerged, lined up at attention and been awarded ribbon medals in order. I came up, nearly a quarter of a mile away; the ceremony had to be restaged. I was given the 1st place medal, down the line adjustments …

On rally Pony Club jamboree lawns of Litchfield hilltop estates and in competitive rings, I cantered, jumped, galloped and gasped in severe asthmatic struggle with horse allergies days at a time – my arms enraged by scarlet blotches when their breath or saliva touched my skin.

A tender, masculine kilted (Scottish American) upper crust patriarch – larger than life itself Mr. Haight – came, knelt beside me and spoke quietly as I struggled with breathing.

"How are you lad?"

A moment, a gentle hand on my forehead.

"You'll be alright son."

How these moments of kindness stay with you.

- until finally, after three, four days and nights my body developed immunity.

And how lucky I was to have these Highland descendants step forth in my life.

I emerged, clear-headed, ready to mount, to fly fields, to collide over fenced water obstacles and logged mud holes.

*****

A finely formed, earthy 18-year-old girl-woman, took me from a dance, allowed us to kiss like hot V8 entangled pistons, batted off tit and pussy advances until finally I surrendered, and then, only then, she opened herself to me with the simple declarative phrase, "I wanted you to know who was in control."

We were lost in body possession for months, with one riveting odd caveat. I wasn't allowed to touch her breasts in any way.

We made love – she taking me inside her - ten feet from her father watching TV in another room; we came in fields and secluded areas of schools, always with her arresting, filament brassiere apparel over really creamy full vanilla mammilla.

One night in a room somewhere, she ritualistically stripped the bra, gave her breasts to me. I discovered the reason for the cloaking. She was so sensitive, the moment I touched one nipple she bolted upright, climbing, her body puncturing the drywall, disintegrating a painting. *I had landed on the living shoals of true, deeply blue oceanic terrain.*

*****

I was sent another angel.

Splitting home, I took a job at fourteen as dishwasher and truck driver for a local summer camp servicing Jewish young people from New York City – no mean feat, one needed to be sixteen to get a license.

I was paid $65 dollars a week, untold riches to a child in '63, with room and board, plus worldly girl and boy camper companions from another planet – the Big Apple.

We played cards a lot during down time - Acey Deucey, Hearts, Poker. I won often with a lot of giggles and early gamesmanship. Nothing like watching a player nibble, a bet on perfectly calculated circumstances, then the tempting pot and cards bite back the probabliities, a stunned loser, the uproar and pot doubling exponentially.

I slept through a raid of the camp by the sub mafia gang searching for me, destroying property, terrorizing the New Yorkers.

I had one day off per week, had to hitch since I couldn't take the truck when not working. I stood by the road, singing "Satisfaction" by the Stones.

A thunderous apparition motorcycle ripped by me, so fast it took two hundred yards for the driver to slow and U-turn. He was golden blond, military crew cut; white T-shirt strained by huge pre-steroid Germanic Comic musculature...blue jeans and biker boots, a living WILD ONE poster archetype.

"Get on", he ordered. I climbed astride, my arms barely able to circumvent his torso. The Angel cranked the accelerator, we shot away, both insane and free in violation of Connecticut's helmet law.

Two miles at high speed, sound and vibration, downward to my downtown, where I knew everyone, top to bottom, new born to elderly, a town wiped out by the river beside the main street during the '55 flood, rebuilt and schizophrenically named the 'Still River' at one end, 'Mad River' at the other.

He stopped at a town crossroads. I dismounted, he thundered away, a stranger in a populace of no strangers.

A month later, I went to a dance in the upstairs of a volunteer fire department station. I was doing restrained James Brown dancing. We all could split and slither.

The sub-mafia leader Joe came in, liquored up. He shoved me, leering, brave with the clarity of the drink.

From somewhere I said, "I'm not going to take it anymore, Joe."

I lash against my torturers, smashing teeth/jawbone ...

He shoved me again. I hit him in the face with the force and speed of an arrived young man, a newly minted MMA scorcher, knocking out two incisors. He staggered, gurgled something with blood and enamel bits, and came at me. I hit him again, rupturing his lips, fragmenting more molars.

He fell away, caught by his hyena subordinates, dragged from the dance floor out the door. I stood there, the air clean, sound of the band gone in the ether of adrenaline coursing through me. I danced again.

In moments, the next level of Mafia arrived ... *sent to chastise.* Pete Della Valle, dark eyes and hair, huge, dangerously sociopathic, twenty-eight years old, came at me. I backed away with nowhere to run.

Suddenly...from where? Blond Biker Angel stepped into the no man's land between Pete and I ... two MEN opposites, light and noir black, Godlike matter & anti-matter, Megalon v Gargantua!

My Angel spoke quietly, with an edge. "You want him? You go through me."

Pete stared at him panther-like, alert. Time truly did hang, neither giant wavered till Pete turned and moved away. Then the Angel was gone, just gone, and I was left alone in a crowd.

Friends grabbed me, hustled me from the firehouse floor, threw me into the trunk of a car and sped away before anything more could happen. A mile down the road they pulled me from the trunk, to the rear seat. We drove at high speed – 80mph, 90, 100 plus.

Behind us, headlights, a fast pursuing vehicle, in less than a minute their car nearly slammed into the rear of ours, forced us to the shoulder.

The older brother of the thug I had hit, John, exited their car. With him was the youngest Shoran brother, Frank.

The Shorans were an entertainingly infamous trio of twenty-something benevolent outlaws separate from the Mafia, equally outside societal parameters but somehow free of organized affiliation.

Good scary souls, they liked me for some reason, Frank particularly. He was all bull brawn and burbling big hearted testosterone. His older brother had on his resume: the killing of an attacker by running him over with a car in a parking lot. When the police went to pick up a Shoran they comically piled six officers into a single squad car - pre-

S.W.A.T. - knowing full well the arrest was going to resemble cornering and hog-tying a young rhino.

Frank Shoran and John ordered my car away, my friends tore off. I was alone on the hyper quiet wood road with two murderers.

"You fucking hit my brother!" John screamed. "I get to hit you!"

Jesus this is fucking sophomoric, I thought. Next to his younger brother against whom I had so recently rebelled and denture demolished, John's build was slight, bony. I said, "Fair enough. You hit me, and it's over, no more after that, feud is done?"

"Yes! I hit you fucker, and it's done".

"Just once, you get to hit him just once, you hit him more than once you get me," said Frank, refereeing the conflict, honoring his responsibilities to the sub mafia and his affection for me.

"Okay," I said, not afraid at all. The older brother of sub Mafia swung, the blow glanced harmlessly off my jaw, no damage.

"Okay, that's it," I said, climbing into their car for a lift downtown.

He swung again, his hand skipped off my skull, and slammed his fist full force into Frank Shoran's poor teeth.

Shoran began to cry, not in weakness, in rage at injustice, betrayal. He grasped the sub mafia older brother, flung him into the vehicle, rasping the door pillar with John's body. Incensed, eyes wet, he took the wheel, ripped away.

I stood alone, aware of crickets, stars and the wonderment of events. I never saw Blond Angel again. I was never again attacked or pursued.

"I have a few questions. If you answer without screaming no one's going to get hurt. You understand?" Bo / PALMERS PICKUP

I drove into the gas station at 2am with a juvenile delinquent buddy to ask for change for cigarettes. Crime of opportunity... on radio, VANILLA FUDGE doing a fab remake of the SUPREMES – *'Set me free why don't you babe...'*

The station seemed vacant.

I prowled around, found the attendant sleeping in a car in the repair bay.

Quietly retreating from him, I went to the register, silently opened the draw, pocketed the bills, $200 plus, walked back out to my car and passenger'... LED ZEPPELIN - *'hangman, hangman, wait a little while '*... exited the station, drove 'round the corner and buried the take.

I circled back, reentered the gas station, nudged the attendant, asked him to break a bill. He stumbled sleepy eyed to the register for my change.

He was immediately shocked that it was empty.

"Did you see anyone around here?" He was bewildered and fearful. "No," I said utterly innocently, "I just drove in."

The cops were called. I was interviewed, answered serenely and authoritatively. I knew nothing, was complimented on being a good citizen and sent on my way.

At that moment I became an actor. I could look in the cop's eyes dead on and lie.

Prior to collecting the loot a week later, my buddy was sent to reform school negating the necessity of a split.

*****

My gas station robbery exhibited not only early skill for performance but the chief qualification for successful criminality ... logical thought with empathetic ability to place oneself in the mind of the investigator, merged with imperative common sense to keep your mouth shut.

... now a precocious newbie criminal developing rules for the outlaw operatic life.

Eighty-five per cent of all criminals are caught because they answer the call we as humans have to boast and share, especially with sexual partners.

Lovers become disgruntled due to perceived or real slight; they exact revenge by ratting out. You don't want to get caught, so go it alone (at least in regard to immediate conversations concerning crime and sin) and keep it that way.

We all - perhaps not psychopaths, sociopaths etc. - have a desire to live in truth with the earthly realm. Choose crime and you must subvert that impulse. At least till the statute of limitations plays out.

Later when I actually became an actor, I embraced similar skills and combined it with imagination. Heady mix ....

*****

I did not know it at the time, but I had learned much of the method behind the curtain covering the noble madness of acting. It isn't rocket science but it does possess steps of both artistry and creation.

There is always fun, communication/dialogue, sexuality and jovial intelligence beneath.

And specific, exact components of work on top of this.

Analogy ...

I am a recreational and competitive shooter, trained by LAPD champions, Navy Seals, Marine Recon.

To shoot a bullet successfully on target, down range, into the 'computer' as police affectionately call the brain of an 'asshole' or (politically correct) 'perpetrator' requires 3 components.

One, 'presentation', clearing the weapon from holster, from behind garments, handgrip, fingers on fingers...

Two, 'sight picture', gazing through the sights rather than at the distant target, both eyes open, vision maxed out to the edges…

Three, 'trigger control', making 'love' to the trigger, smooth ascension of pressure, no anticipation of recoil jerking, visualizing the weapon is empty…

Anything less than mastery of all three and one would not accurately strike the target.

And so, I began to discover acting has five components, perhaps six. These components would become my trenches, work that must be done in each and every instance of acting.

*****

For me, the first thing that I learned that is a component of acting is something I call LANDSCAPE.

The more personal and specific my performance, my landscape, the more truthful, powerful and intricate would become my performance – in criminality, athletics or down the road when acting.

Suddenly I knew the seeds of the latter need to make each item in the script, every movement and person, location and time, every item, real, personal and specific.

How did I do that? If the first line of script says, Interior Cell - Day, followed by "Fred hands a bribe to the guard at the door" a great deal is revealed.

Limited actors barely absorb this, saying mentally, I'll wait for my lines. The difference between that dim dilettante effort and the actor who is going to get the job, who is going to make the crew hold their breath, stop and watch as they perform is significant.

First, where is this cell? I make it a real cell or space I know intimately.

I've got the bills and I hand them to the guard, and it's the cash I procured from the robbery when I was 14 years old, I know the denomination, the number of 5's, 10's, 20's … $200 total for the gas station half pint heist.

Here's the back story to make that guard personal and specific for me: Forgive me, what I'm about to say, "but I fucked the guard's wife." His name's Miguel and I slept with his wife last week just as I slept with the German diplomat's wife, and it becomes for me as personal and specific as the Spanish woman with her red head sister, and I'm giving him exactly $200 *in pesos*, and he knows everything because he's one of the duo sent to turn my young body to a bag of broken bone glass.

The answer to every question becomes yes. This heightens the stakes, splashes action and word with nuance. Yes, he knows I've played with the texture of his wife's opened beckoning sex. Yes, the cop at the gas station knows I stole the dough.

Making it personal … Miguel isn't a mythical guard. Miguel becomes the diplomat, who lives with the wife with whom I dallied, my chippie partner with the voyeuristic sister.

Yes, I made it richly personal and colored.

I'm wearing the suit that indicates my part, and I'm complete, ready to dance, for all drama and crime is a dance of death and much is psycho sexual, great acting to some measure comes from the seductive, laughing hard cock and the open, eternally captivating pussy. These forces have given rise and toppled nations, initiated war and duels, caused the fusion of madness and mirth – all very human and universal.

The perversion of this can and has been used by sexual manipulators and predators of the entertainment industry – teachers, directors, actors alike. But the eradication of these impulses, their rightful power and free rein, by potential excesses from #metoo does not serve either art or actors.

What is required is easy acceptance of the actual steamy, salacious to divine (or repression of venereal to sacred) underpinnings of drama and comedy with a respect for both language and presentation in the discussion and demo. It is not for the lightweight but for the brave – those who revel in worldly immersion.

Is it any wonder that acting classes are now top source of #metoo claims – insurers ran for the hills, leaving drama, art schools of all persuasions where?

How can one discuss performance without clenching racism, war, Mommy and Daddy's death, vigilante massacres ad infinite … pillars plus of all since Greeks were espousing democracy and butt holing pages?

Shakespeare takes the hand of humanity and reveals hearts and noble esprit of Abbott & Costello grave diggers to usurping kings.

All the topics our new thin ice neo puritanical society deems 'uncomfortable making'. Couple this cretinously PC cold brew with the sprawling potpourri of damaged half-wits drawn to thespian land and the pit of delusion called Hollywood.

*****

The casting people, producers and directors watching me in the decades to come, are going to know an accomplished actor within seconds of the beginning of an audition or scene. The lesser actor is not going to get this, not going to know the LANDSCAPE, so they're going to sit down and they're going to start the scene plainly with only lines and no intricately personal/specific LANDSCAPE, and they won't have made it their own - the prison, the cell, potent and perfect.

I would know the diplomat Miguel has bad breath, reeking of elk sausage. I will know because I build and take from the very elaborate essence of my life.

Now, I will not always consciously think about all of these things, but I inject all that alchemy into my crimes and later my performances, before authority, the law, the audience, like a twinkling light as air paper creation I throw into the

132

air, as I am doing it, wisps and scraps of imagination floating about me like tiny individual droplets of white pearl cum and spewing female juices.

All of it as I live in the moment.

If the second line is "He takes his seat opposite the prisoner Carlos" - I take my seat. I tap my tie as cum and snowflakes drift, moisten and soften. I take my glasses and clean them with my tie, a snowflake has fallen upon the lens.

And Carlos, across from me, is someone real, I have already written on the left side of my script exactly who Carlos is, his name, his very being.

By the way, I'm going to make him slightly left center of my gaze. I'm going to place him in the LANDSCAPE of my 'V'. You see, I form a V from me to the camera, because if I'm acting outside the V then no one – not the cop, not the casting director, not the audience - can see my performance, for vastly and generally, without my eyes there is no performance.

If Eva, a young Sophia Loren, enters from the left of the V she will always enter from the left of the V. And I will know exactly who she is, the color of her lips and the tincture of her kiss, all of it drawn from my life escapades.

The guy/gal Carlos, that I'm going to have most of my lines with - directly in front of me - I would put them as the casting director reading opposite me, and place them right there at the very center of the V. The video camera taping me for transmission to the decision makers is going to be right there within the V, perhaps slightly right center.

For what do you think a director, casting director or producer is looking for when anyone auditions or acts? They won't articulate it as this but they are looking for skill in utilizing imagination, looking for someone to create and embody a being for the 21st century, as intently as a cop looking for a scoundrel picking up lucre from a gas station till.

This is flat-out important in the age of 'green screen' computer graphics (CGI). BRAVEHEART, 300, TROY, SAVING PRIVATE RYAN, the new SPARTACUS, GLADIATOR, GAME OF THRONES to name just a tiny fraction of shows, all animation (this includes all voiceover work as well) – nothing is there to act against or with, save your ability to imagine.

Including some battery dead dildo international lead actors - THE NAMES - who can't summon minimal discipline to learn lines or even use cue cards because of fallen lack of character and craft. Actors, will find themselves 'acting' with a 'star' void, a sad sack of indulgence and organic brain damage. Better to be opposite a lighting pole with a scribbled smiley face scotch taped to the shaft with one's own imagination than opposite the drugged, selfish and deranged.

Am I being cruel? Perhaps, plus a measure of righting the ship of state. There are too many heroes in daily life – firemen, single mothers and fathers, wounded warriors, quiet instruments of human courage to do anything but call out those who take without craft and passion.

There is often nothing except my power over my own work, my command and skill in any audition or performance. My ability to fly and dominate space with ease and vibration.

After all, one must in auditions, conjure romanticism with a casting person male or female who may resemble an un-lanced boil.

They aren't looking for someone with whom to shake hands, they aren't looking for 'serviceable' acting. They may be prowling for physical wow and striking bone structure or extreme, scarred ugliness but these are secondary.

They're primarily looking for the 'truth', the 'choices' and the 'presence' ... unique professional mastery, individual creation, someone who has done the work and knows, loves, embraces, claws, jigs in the LIGHT OF THE LANDSCAPE.

A criminal who can flash before them and escape leaving only a sense of laughter and wonder.

They are looking for Brando (before the fall), one who knows where the gas station attendant sleeps, where the unmarked bills lie, who can replicate gentle seduction of the sliding cash register draw. Each is looking to fall in love with wild innocent eyes of the boy or girl, man or woman, cock and pussy who looks confidently and serenely into the

face of Law Enforcement and lies their enchanting lines
and lives in the moment of fire.

Eleven: Mortality Fanfare

"Those were our orders sir.
Children, let's go!
There are mountains to the east and west, which
means they have to come through this ravine to get
to us." Reese / STAR TREK DEEP SPACE NINE

Images of high school - coupling as lovers and drinking gin
to the point of puking evergreen essence at a 'death
descent' ski resort called 'Satan's Ridge', street drag
racing ourselves and the pursuing cops... driving 70mph
backwards 'round darkened lake roads ... football,
basketball, baseball, walking country ditches with a double
barreled side by side shotgun I inherited when its 19-year-
old owner used it to blow his head off in suicide.

I was suspended for several games from the baseball team
when my mother reported me for smoking Marlboros to her
lover, my baseball coach.

A first ex-girlfriend was parked in an idling station wagon,
in the dead of crisp winter, sprawled, offering herself to her
new boyfriend, not knowing the exhaust pipe was backed
into a snow bank, carbon monoxide injecting into the car.
They fell asleep forever, hands on breasts and faces,
mouths on lips and skin, ensnared in death.

I kicked off, ran for touchdowns, made interceptions and
terminating tackles, primary colored days and artificially lit
greenish blue Friday nights as wide receiver and
linebacker, stormed the backboard in compressed gym
cacophony reverberating basketball games, seventy two

rebounds in one game … hitting cleanly on baseball diamonds from one small Connecticut town to another, studied French, committing felonies now and then … set a school record of two thousand sit ups in one go, judged fastest runner in the school by elimination contests.

And like Big Dick Height post alcohol, we hellions circumvented Highland Lake seeking adrenaline and thrills.

Driving the local body of fresh water rear bumper first, neck cranked round, turning rear view window into wind shield, the one handed reverse steer, other arm draped over seat.

One by one, round hairpin curves sheathed by color mad maple and omnipresent pine in fall, or white and black spotted birch winters, road dry then slick with ice waiting in hollow dips and valleys of asphalt made colder by plump, snow weighted verdant trees … others stripped clean.

Month of May jade wet buds dripping ice … Harry Winston diamonds and emeralds on an aging beauty's wrists and upper body, cover girl once more.

The view from the vehicle: one tree, another, another, flitting by, best at night so oncoming headlights give warning, kamikaze by day.

Pursuit of time, seven minutes, seven miles.

A side dish of absurdist daredevil ditz in a stolen shopping cart towed by a long, leonine rope and a Volkswagen bus, on a deserted 'under construction' freeway to nowhere, eight of us onboard. We crashed when we tried to push it to 82mph, hit a patch of sand, somersaulting and giggling, miraculously unscathed.

*****

Teenagers die.

In Connecticut, the converging of two sets of liquor laws conspired against the young. New York's age of consumption then eighteen, Connecticut's twenty-one.

Across the rural NY border a boom town of bars arose, for kid crowds running GTOS, Vettes, Challengers, Road Runners – blistering expressions of MUSCLE auto culture – child athletes, teenage demon angels became paralyzed and worse as inevitable crashes occurred.

Twenty-seven, snap-of-the-fingers miles from Winsted Main Street to the opportunistic bar boomtown district of Millerton, New York. Speed records were set going up, catastrophes and youth guillotine annihilation fueled by blood level liquor ruin coming back – Gary Fecto, Jimmy Guerard, Jones, Leslie – names, young dead beauties, annals of tragedy.

Friday night at the Shell station was prime liturgy of the Eucharist – the altar where wrecks, vinyl and windshields flecked with brain and hair, were towed in.

Dazzled and beguiled by each showing I came regularly – our lives weekly terminal splatter theater as many in my hometown were speared or maimed.

Nearby was Tony's – gathering hole diner, sausages and grilled chops, fist fights, projectile upchuck and male lingering after drive-in sex, distilled chromatic – stupid to splendid - profane 'nightcap' dialogue.

Crashes and casualties never slacked our appetite for olive oiled corkscrew penne or marinara shells, white-on-white fountain malted confections.

So good morning after the nights of our mortality ... teenage breakfast on athlete days: oat bran flax Buckwheat pancakes, grain flakes and walnuts, thick cream milk, whisked, topped with fresh picked blueberries, strawberries ... a medallion of Toronto pepper crusted sirloin ... hot, black French roasted coffee smell, adults sipping only ... nutmeg and lamb sausage ...

Into the afternoon early evening flowering of my athletic performer life before crowds and collective adoration ... becoming 'known'... able to walk into rooms with positive fore-knowledge of your expertise and being ... drawing the cheerleading princesses to my body and the hatred and admiration of nearby town opposing champions.

Night time make-outs and teenage carnage, braying drunken cannibal comic celebrants of each other's intimate yet publicly consumed small town lives ...

Fights ... I stood there, shirt ripped by opponents' finger as they went down ... without animosity, safely wondering, sensuous and combatively immortal even when next door the body parts of families and children lay splashed across junkyard remains.

Love this picture of my father. Direct, suspender not exactly symmetrical, bow tie slightly askew. So much of social media modern life is curated to be over perfect. Wish you were around to chat Dad.

Perhaps we should reconsider contraception ...

ROBERT D. KILPATRICK, JR.
JR.
"Killer"   College
"Man can be destroyed but not de-
feated."

Hemingway

old school cool

turn Rebel loose ...

Speed, exhilaration, freedom, disciplined recklessness and a great place to muse over the loss of virginity.

Suck my balls Dressage People...

Prom ... despite two provocative pom-poms on her rabbit stole she never let me slide into home base.

Twelve: Crash and Vectoring

"With what we stand to gain, they're acceptable losses."
Duke 'Free-fall' Fontaine / TOUR OF DUTY

It was my turn.

At 17, in full expanding expression as a high school athlete, I exploded my spine in a car crash.

I see that night as a culmination of mad motorcycles, junk vehicles stripped down to their engine essentials so that all each did was burn out, roar silly away from the police. Madcap along rural roads, airborne over spillways, a long poem of speed, risk and abandon.

I became the lamb, Friday night sacrifice, on team curfew, a football game next day … obligated to be in bed by 10pm as a rising captain. I went downtown to mill around by the Cathedral wall, to 'hang', to commune amidst teenage action.

Still in glow of new found acceptance as an athlete, a wider realm of friends admiring me, lauding me, I was flattered when the varsity team captain Denny glided up in his car.

"Want to go to the line to pick up JoAnn?" JoAnn, his girlfriend whom I admittedly adored. I jumped in the passenger seat. He drove too quickly to New York. He went in the Tallyho Tavern, I remained in the car. He returned to the car an hour later. I fell asleep against the passenger door as we drove homeward in the time of no seatbelts.

146

Miles down the road the car's violent skidding awoke me. The world was sliding, there was a boom crack of split metal and glass as the passenger door was torn off, sheared away by hard raking impact with the steel railing of a bridge.

Car gyrated wickedly, rushing forward at eighty, tires tearing sideways for nearly a quarter mile.

My body was flung about, darkness and indistinct imagery everywhere … an upward impetus as the car left the highway and climbed the forty-five-degree hillside, an abrupt explosive blackout as the vehicle collided head on with a huge boulder painted with the letter G in bright gold and blue, there was a white-hot skull flash and I was gone.

Very pulpy, very James Dean, mid-century SFX, speeding violently into the giant symbol of our high school north above the town. I was a Gilbert School Yellow Jacket even in calamity.

I came awake to sounds sometime after being knocked out by the crash, either flung out of the ripped off door or catapulted through the shattered windshield, eyes crusted blind by sand and blood.

Voices about me, "There goes the football team", a girl muttered.

Denny was unscathed.

I saw only occasional lights. Like a thousand times before, locals gathered to witness and offer benediction to the gore. I was loaded unseeing into an ambulance, transported in expanding agony to a small hospital, cleaned up on an operating slab, lying unmoving as a corpse, paralyzed.

My body had jackknifed so violently a vertebra was shattered, pinching the spinal cord. My father arrived to stand at my side, gazing down at me, whispering "You really messed yourself up this time son." As a father of sons myself now I can imagine his anguish.

He then went to work for me, rushing to my aid with will and resources, found the best surgeon available, the boldest techniques and most brilliantly accessible contemporary facility.

I was driven by ambulance 60 miles to Hartford Hospital – a teaching hospital - each second a matrix of brutal pain from my back and legs, every pebble of the road transmitting knife fire to my spine.

I lay face contorted, in the rotating light of the rolling injury bay. X-rays revealed an entire vertebra – T12 – burst.

Descending into opiate unconsciousness, I was operated on by 4am. Three wires were implanted from the vertebra above the damaged to the one below the imploded bone – stabilizing the area, an early form of mobile fusion.

My parents, god love them, were taken to breakfast by the surgeon the morning after the accident and told I might never walk again.

*****

This would not be my final crash.

I survived a series of fiery, bone cracking crashes, cars & motorcycles. Naked & gored upon the parkway… pretty scenery & landscapes throughout.

If a script contains a motorcycle, it's not merely a 'motorcycle' but the red 1978 Moto Guzzi 850 Le Mans with a shaft drive that let me wear a tuxedo around Manhattan with a model named Leila on board, delectable body crushed to my back - no oil spitting up on my James Bond attire, shaft drive rather than messy chain, torque left of the machine in the direction of the engine revolution tilting us left ever so persuasively, so quiet and smooth I could sneak up on others.

I totaled the Moto Guzzi *wearing only silk pajamas, Viet Cong sandals and a Bell Star helmet* in a wreck on the Saw Mill River Parkway at 60mph after smoking a joint, my eyes turning blue post making love to my first ex-wife one last time and then many times with a new Israeli lover – so tired I fell asleep, waking up an inch from the curb and somersaulting on impact – huge sash of flame and chrome on asphalt sparks, barreling over and over, arriving nude, filaments of wardrobe shorn and imbedded in the road rash, a fractured bone protruding from my hand.

One handed I wasn't able to take off the helmet.

I was heating up, going foggy into shock inside the Plexiglas shield, bloody skin missing from my entire left side just deep enough to be a source of weeping agony that would last for weeks.

Cars scattered, pulled over to avoid the burning wreckage. A woman approached, ludicrously her eyes roving from my helmeted head to my dangling genitalia. I would survive, internally I chuckled at the notion of her squeamish trembling, all was not lost, my cock could still cause a stir.

"Could you help me with the chin strap?" I said softly. "Otherwise, I may vomit inside the helmet." She did and I lay down, stayed still till EMT men lifted me away, past crash and fire ruined noble machine.

Later, there was the Harley 1200 chopper with extended 8-foot fork leaping from my control, gas tank detonating on the family lawn as the entire clan gathered to welcome me back from university, *gone for 2 years I was now arriving in a motorized fireball.*

Swathed in a huge Canadian Maple Leaf flag stolen from the police station outside Toronto's Strawberry Fields Rock Festival – northern version of Woodstock – journeying with gear, buddys and an elfin demi-size Botticelli cutey named Antoinette, who kissed me for a thousand miles, then racing all day against all manner of diabolical and outlandish machines on the venue's Grand Prix track, bathing in hallucinations and manifestations of music by night.

There is a dynamic rationale for my wandering among these cataclysmic incidents.

There is nothing ambiguous in my remembering as an actor … no difficulty in the assignment of personal and specific color to every object, word, locale, person or action in any script.

Friends, characters, relatives, employed for unique traits, passions and foibles to enrich emotional and dramatic worlds.

Buxom, insanely buoyant hi-decibel Kathy Guerard, 'Cool Hand Luke' Buddy Ouellette, mad egoist, b-ball dribbler bully 'Pinky' Bunel, Lynn Attella and Rita DiGiovanni kissing me, tousling and swatting away my roving fingers … Craig Centrella, Jon Weber, Sal Harrington, Jim Fecto, Brian Bagnall, Frank McGuire, Irene, Dorothy and Jimmy Connole – all joker fabulous kids, who came by school bus to the hospital after the car wreck, high and wild mates beside me in high school and later others, in college, F. Alan Fankhanel, Larry Caldwell and John Bishop, all on insane covert and illegal endeavors.

The drunk driver team captain Denny, never came to visit, without judgment or malice, coward? wastrel? … he never comes perhaps because he couldn't face his weakness, having twisted another human being, he received only a sprained wrist from the wreck. What he doesn't know is the wreck was favor from the Almighty.

All these matchless creatures swimming in my mental reservoir to be called upon for clear paintings of pain and pleasure.

*****

The reason I write all these landscape components, people, objects and locations down on the left side of my script page is because when I go away to a movie or dinner with a friend, or lover or whomever, or go to teach another class, coach another actor, or bathe my child, then as I come back to the material, I quickly go through these highlights, humans and memories and I've got the whole scene mapped, an entire emotional 'War and Peace' front and center again in my head.

I give myself a gift, lovely color wrapped, by reading these notes, signs and memories quietly with focus on the page.

Then I can play in a zone of perfection rather than a neural pattern littered with mistakes.

And I do that every single time, each audition and performance, each time using the mortar of Landscape and Memorization, *remembering* - nutrient rich, fertile.

Thirteen: More Mad Memory

"You're not afraid of flying are you? Because when we get up nice and high, I want to drop you right on top of this building." Paul Masters / SHARK

When I awoke after back surgery, housed in intensive care, I had three peerless traumatized and damaged roommates.

Diagonally across from me was a neck broke Irish brawler laid low. A 7&7 beer chaser bruiser, he had been involved in a bar fight, had made others pay until they threw him down a flight of stairs, transforming him in an instant from street fighter to helpless new born quadriplegic – life without movement.

The medical team had drilled his skull, placed hooks in his cranium to alleviate pressure on his neck. He was on his back, a large leather, and polished tube apparatus encasing his head – a nightmarish steam punk rat hat contraption. All below the break was now forever still - toes, calves and thighs, cock, hands, arms, triceps, biceps, gone, only memories of agility and potencies.

Saliva would gather in his mouth. Incapable of turning sideways even with his neck, unable to depress the ringer button with helpless fingers, spit slowly garbling his speech as he began to cry for the nurse to drain his mouth

"Nurse, nurth, nur, nur!" They never came. In helplessness, he would gob straight up toward tiny holes in the acoustic ceiling, phlegm going up, then falling straight back down into his own face.

The cycle would begin again, then again, repeating endlessly.

Directly across from me was a ginger youth, 'Mute Boy,' large, violently induced scar in his throat carved below a head shaved after cranial surgery. A car crash participant as well, the steering wheel had pierced ruptured his throat rendering him speechless all his earthly time.

Sentences meted out here are rather harsh!

In the bed next to me caged Octogenarian 'Grandfather Ole Man River', certainly in his eighties, hands burned and hugely bandaged. His sole Alzheimer quest was to escape his bandages, which in dementia he viewed as unjust constraints.

It would often take him up to a week to disengage himself from the bandages, nurses catching him just at the treasure of freedom.

Caregivers would then escalate the restraint, tying him down, placing thick chord netting over his bed. He'd go to work again, unraveling gauze and cords, plucking at knots, cutting net links with his teeth, a week, two, of diligent bright-eyed effort, only to be caught and halted at the star moment of completion.

And me (plummeting wounded boy) ...

My choreography went like this: at the starting line, I received an intravenous shot of morphine; instantly ascended into a languid, pain-free 'joy' cocoon of 60 deeply-drugged minutes.

The second hour, all high evaporating but pain not yet returned, a calm but wary normalcy; third hour, teeth-gritting, bolting, fire pain sweeping in, dominating all aspiration and circumstance; fourth hour a pastiche of agonized bursts of weeping, not an hour but lifetime seconds, minutes, eternities, retching forward until the next arrival of a nurse bearing another liquid laden heaven needle.

When they were anything but unwaveringly punctual, it became a horrid, deeply personal betrayal, a selfish war crime against me.

In an effort to keep me from developing bedsores, I was turned in two hour increments. This was conducted with an apparatus developed for Teddy Kennedy after he broke his back in a plane crash – a Stryker frame.

The Stryker consists of two bed halves, top and bottom. I'm lying face down much like on a present-day chiropractor's bench, staring at the floor through a split, two hours, catching white matronly shoes moving in my peripheral orbit, then the top half is wheeled in, placed on top, bonds strapped and tightened, a handle, *like priming an early propeller*, is cranked, tossing me over, now I'm facing upward. The top half is lifted off and rolled away until the next two hours passes. Now I gaze at the beehive acoustic ceiling.

I fitfully slept, never to REM. Awakened by bowel movements and bed pan changing, catheter insertion, clockwork Stryker chorus or the ever-coming dissipation and revival of morphine, the occasional rookie rotund nurse arriving after midnight, gaily grabbing my foot, "How ya doin?"

I screamed, writhed in pain at the touch. Dark, novice nurse angels with iridescent pearl teeth in the night, no way of knowing the currents coursing always in my savaged nerve pathways.

A blessing ...

Fourteen: Arise

"There's no way out Kate. My nightmare! My rules! No matter where you go!" Conrad Phibes/ SLEEPWALKERS

Never to walk again, never to fuck again, never to achieve my strong body above a woman I love, triceps, biceps, hips and back descending with power … fuck that, not likely.

Never to hunt and fish, never to shoot an elk with a pistol at 120 yards and boar herds from a helicopter, never to boat trout in Montana, execute 'speed goat' antelope in Wyoming.

To only exist from a wheelchair, never to have children, *save extracted centrifuge implantation and who would want weak, dissipate sperm*, never to rock them as I sing away their tears, never to play international rugby on hypnotic Caribbean islands, never to walk and work among media titans and fashion icons of New York, never to rise up, to do cinema war with nearly every leading man in the world of movies, never to celebrate the arsenal of small arms and pugilistic arts.

Not once to climb a peak in Colorado and look down from a mountain at approaching Pompeii-like, billowing snowstorms below.

Never to go to Afghanistan, Dubai, Uzbekistan, Kyrgyzstan to meet brave and brilliant Coalition warriors, never to glory in war choppers, dangling over prehistoric plateaus and primordial mountain ranges, never to be airborne over the Andes in an Avianca flight crammed with sheep, flailing chickens and terror-stricken children, never carousing with Cartagena teenagers with AK-47 knockoffs in their City of Ancient Genocidal Gold … *a long never for anyone.*

I didn't become a paraplegic. The writhe inducing pain (an unceasing birth to death series of gift blessings for me) *means that not only are the nerves not entirely dead,* but destiny is smiling on this tearful frail male biped. A tiny sliver fraction away from severed spine …

Orthopedic specialists have looked at my x-rays, MRIs – have burst into laughter …

Two weeks later in swept a nurse with a tiny white cup containing a pair of pills. I was stripped of the morphine and the needles, sobbing in despair, yes (I knew those fucking pills wouldn't compare to Lady Sweet fluid) … *necessary weaning to prevent addiction.*

Two months after that, after not peeing on my own without a tube the entire time, not walking to a single meal, waiting for the metronomic clockwork of delivered trays and pharmaceuticals, I was swathed in a body cast from chin to groin, able to rise from the Stryker, muscle mass gone, atrophied, stumble to the bathroom down the hall, blessedly no more defecating in a pan placed under my ass by a nurse, an end to deliciously being washed by serving others.

I found a wheelchair, created balancing tricks with it, transformed the thing into a circus racing vehicle, whipping down black and white linoleum floored halls, flirting with nurses as they bend near me, their eyes, smells and bodies transcendent hallucinogens.

I went to a half way facility, offshoot of the hospital. The mere act of moving from one room to another to eat with others was despairingly difficult.

I was sent home in a week, half better equipped but struggling. Going up a flight of stairs seemed impossible. My father standing outside the room as I wept after achieving the top, gently speaking, "Are you alright son? I know it's hard."

I returned to school, young girls who had known me in my athletic bloom would say kindly, "You look better thin." They were lying.

I was wasted, relearning to walk with asymmetrical nerve damage of my legs, saying goodbye to jock persona, watching others become captains or MVP's, painfully apart from sport glories of wide skies and cheering crowds, no steak and egg pre-game breakfasts, no nascent power, no fastest young man in the school, instead an inexplicably clumsy team-less being.

I arose four months later, and in the next ten years, rehabilitated to the point of doing my own stunts in a multitude of films and television shows.

Ascent from ambulatory pit ...

The street fighter was still there when I left the hospital. While still in the cast I took on three hammered Torrington bullies who jumped me one night – followed them down, beat them with my fists, one per week, sustaining colorful blackened eyes, high school crowd gazing at idiots.

The drive of a teenage daredevil, body of a still-weakened cripple – without muscle, calves unsightly, wholly gone - warrior without realm in which to exalt.

Denied sports for a decade - my 'reason for being' - exploded along with my vertebra, inarticulate like most young jocks, I wrote to communicate *(and earn spending coin)* with the world in the 10-year journey to physical resurrection. I communed ever more with a lifetime of influential literary masters & their deviant/noble characters.

I became a writer, so as I arrived at acting I possessed the body of an athlete once more, but with senses for literature and rhythmic language, culture born of ads, journalism, theater.

Fuck I'm happy when I'm learning ... Life is education and empathy.

It was a heady, versatile mélange, ideally suited to entertainment. You see, once again, 'bad' or 'inconvenient' event was the positive pivot of God's will to an ultimate dream.

The divine intelligence knows what we want/need before we even imagine.

160

Fifteen: Literacy Before Flight
"Bring me a dream Burke. Bring me a dream."
Christian 'The Sandman' Naylor / DEATH
WARRANT

I never wanted nor even conceived of being an actor. I didn't know what one was. My dreams, like many young men, were absorbed first in living life to the full and simply getting laid. My book stars led their lives with a lawless unruly poise and exuberance that held me, tickled me.

Even when banned from watching the broadcasts, I clandestinely watched movies and television at home as a child - original Kirk Douglas SPARTACUS or John Wayne SANDS OF IWO JIMA, DISNEY'S JULES VERNE'S 20,000 LEAGUES UNDER THE SEA, westerns and war noir patriotic flicks of American preeminence and man's innate striving for nobility, courage and value codes … early 3 channel television – HONEYMOONERS, LUCY, action serials, etc. When parental controlled risqué bits aired – I ran the picture mute on the small television in my room, relying on the sound wafting up from downstairs where the parents viewed.

W.C. Fields and Laurel & Hardy sent me into wild laughter. Still do.

Later I lived and grew up at Drive-In movies, sneaking 18 teenagers in the trunk, fighting, drinking, making love, vandalizing speakers – tearing away with ripped braided chords dangling from all four windows.

None of this foundational image factory output ever gave rise to any vocational desire on my part or awareness of entertainment entities beyond the 'tube' or screen, through the drive-in windshield or ahead on paths of projected light – in delight of the deep darkened cushy classicism 30's art deco theaters.

Performers enacting these myths simply were there. They weren't admired by me; they simply existed as backdrop for my grovels.

Years later Olivier, Laughton, Guinness, Mason and Gielgud, Burton to Brando and Lee Marvin would join Rimbaud, Morrison and Bowie to jig within the influencing flock.

Sixteen: Fire Images

"People die. Once you get passed that the object is to win." Duke 'Free-fall' Fontaine / TOUR OF DUTY

In the tumultuous collegiate days of '68-'72, there was no 'physical therapy,' only two football players and myself hardening our non-verbal selves with iron in the University of Richmond (U of R) gym.

USA was incendiary with racial riots, anti-Viet Nam revolt, feminism flaring, divisions never even considered in my equalitarian New England childhood.

Washington D.C., 90 miles away, was aflame with protest at the war.

California and the Left beyond – San Francisco to Paris - were then whitewashing Mao/Che/North Viet Nam/Viet Cong/Fidel's butcheries to stupor romanticism. It's here we see the gory alien chest bursting birth of today's headlong continuum of Hollywood Left spin mashing any good idea – Chicano rights over the years twists into grotesquely colossal illegal immigration/open borders/ sanctuary cities for criminals, sexual identity freedom is seized as rationale for children drugged to gender morphing, voter rights equates to no need for ID to prove legal residence (much less citizenship), social safety net becomes living wage/welfare fraud and 50 million food stamp recipients, free speech becomes hate speech and fair game for violent rioting, healthcare is mandated irrespective of any sustainable economic model, glory be to any authoritarian socialist experiment despite their global failure ... any divergent viewpoint becomes racism, fascism, Nazism, women's rights becomes a cudgel of man hate, unionism alters from warriors of labor to blockers of quality education and competition or worse funders of entrenched corruption, legitimate and long due #metoo cleansing spins into a slide of manipulative PR and suppression of women's and men's voices of commonsense and appreciation, animal rights becomes eradication of managed resource hunting, the Feminist Left never met a Muslim they didn't like while staying mute to international female oppression by Islam and decrying Christian religious freedom if it runs counter to any LBGT sprawl. No matter the noble cause and its inception – Hollywood and the Leftie Coasts have poured on a cavalcade of weirdness and thought dictatorship upon the chasms in the country.

Much to their own diminishment. Millions of people throughout the nation could care less for the breathtaking insights of the entertainment class.

I voted for Clinton twice (almost went to work for his election) – before he was a revealed rapist and on camera national Lewinsky liar, before he and Gore started giving blow-jobs to the Red Chinese Army via $4m in a bag from a Buddhist Temple. I then voted for Bush "W" twice which was fab – the only President that sent me $1600 in tax cuts when I needed it to feed my children and only military leader in human history who conquered Afghanistan with the loss of only 141 troops.

I gave Obama a chance to govern, voted for the loquacious traitor, hoped for energy and purpose, got treason, hell I might have voted for Hillary had not Benghazi burned and illuminated the trail of high crimes, misdemeanors and global graft engulfing that witch.

One doesn't have to be a Pulitzer Prize winning journalist to see the fetid trail leading to that particular rats nest in the fumes of the DNC.

'Liberals in name only' never gave Trump a moment of bonhomie, never bestowed anything but bile, hysterical angst.

And he's still wiping the floor with your heaped-on hate and transforming the world.

The TRUMP SHOW – the New York, builder tough man with grit and balls ... course you Lefties aren't feeling the Trump Remake.

The hunchback in 300, at least had injustice visited upon him, you ill liberals have not - you abdicate soul and patriotism, to betray and whine ...

The saving ... only half the population buys the bilge.

*****

1968 college life collided with brutal televised imagery of Viet Nam, nefarious politics and cultural schism, militarized tactical police, spellbinding Hendrix led rock and roll, the deeply saddening, riot inducing deaths of Martin Luther King and Robert Kennedy.

Came together like the impaling sabers of a Custer and Stuart charge in the rear battle corridor of Gettysburg - bodies pierced twenty yards deep on either side.

In the inner city, people of color flamed their own neighborhoods, looted in utter frustration and futile, perpetrating in perpetuity self-destruction. Black Panthers arose and were murdered, misguided petulant Weathermen lashed out in terrorism.

As I write this, I watch ROBERT KENNEDY for PRESIDENT on NETFLIX – so obvious that Robert Kennedy must have known it was almost certainly coming after MLK went down. He must have had so much courage to proceed knowing ... each time he touched his children, smiled at his wife, saw a sunset ...

... many were left with the inescapable certainty - Jesus to Gandhi to John Lennon, one who stands for universal love, a different expression of earthly humanity will certainly be struck down. Still we go forth ... are you pig, coward or a warrior of Olympian decency, heart and empathy?

We are all on a suicide run – best to make the most of it – only game in town.

I attended//graduated University of Richmond as father, mother did before me, sister, brother following. My parents had married in the chapel cathedral. It made them happy to see me go to U. of R. and wishing them happy, so I did, to my betterment.

Richmond, the birthplace of American Revolution, Patrick Henry's "Give me liberty of give me death!", deeply anti-Federal capital of the Confederacy, was as I stumbled arrived rainbow enmeshed in cultural inflammation and chaotic amalgams. Jews, blacks, juice head footballers, pre & explosive hippie artistry (the city was a flowery seat of counterculture dating back to the 30's through the Beatnik era), freewheeling flowing music - Redding to James Brown, Airplane, Tina Turner, Eastern psychedelic student secession – *idealism fun forward.*

It cost my parents and me $1500 per semester - room, board and tuition. Thank you, Faye and Bob – heartfelt.

U of R is now the most expensive university in Virginia. Today, an out-of-state student pays $54,000 plus per year and climbing.

To pick up cash I became a jubilant guinea pig junkie for Big Pharma - volunteered for emerging drug studies launched by A. H. Robbins Pharmaceuticals. Robbins himself a U. of R. grad and was grateful to the school. He put his substantial money where his head and body had been. The new gym I restored myself in was part of a fine athletic center funded by and named after Robbins.

The company maintained a nearby research facility. $60 per hour I cheekily submitted to gagging down clear plastic throat tubes connected to baskets of egg white suspended in my stomach (measuring protein absorption), swallowing rollout muscle relaxants and opening my arm for injections of scrubbed heroin Demerol, an early version of cleaned up morphine.

An electrode was attached to my ear by white coated lab staff; electric current sent burning through my lobe, rising to painful level.

When I couldn't stand it any longer, I depressed a cut-off switch in my hand. A baseline pain threshold established, a mute syringe bearing lab tech entered, shot me up, current again pulsed into my ear, pain now completely masked by the drug.

I would pass out from Demerol high, wake up hours later, pleasantly alone in the hospital, richer by a couple hundred dollars, ear pulsing and scarlet, swollen from uninterrupted current. I let myself out into the fresh Virginia night.

I loved the easy lucre. It bolstered my supplemental food shoplifting – I was partial to Porter House steak. Standard new swinging butt plug college idiocy.

One day a supermarket clerk became suspicious of me wearing a winter artic infantry coat in sweltering spring Richmond - it took just a single foot chase out of a Piggly Wiggly to halt my 5-finger discount behavior.

I know when to get out when getting is good, the concept of pushing one's luck beyond the big benevolence in the sky.

The essential difference between my brother and I seemed to be his lifelong inability to 'skate' from youth transgressions and my great propensity for not getting caught as I was allowed me to 'mature'.

I walked. He got caught.

His stumbles had to do with base line silliness of idiot crimes, the frenzy of his substance indiscipline ... my early embrace of delicacy and clever movement.

A portion of his troubles and my successes (escapes) resided also with sheer luck and parental energy. My parents were quite hardcore with me. More moneyed and indulgent with him. This laxity to him didn't serve him.

I was an unrepentant roustabout, yes, a perfectly happy one, but also never desirous of creative repetition. Exude general good spirit, dine and dash, one time raid sensibility. Establish no patterns, maintain alternate paths of deniability and the 'cute' un-sweating chops to feign innocence or plucky misunderstanding.

A 'cock' tail of tap dancing naughty entertainment jock poet boy.

Some of my delinquent cohorts ended up in reform school, prison, worse – I went on to college and beyond, half individual drive, half preordination.

*****

American society, the city of Richmond *and the college* were a brew of several strains of incompatible flow. Drunken bulbous white supremacists in madras shorts moved in easy lockstep with the black horn section big band spectacle, drifting beside a Thai stick enhanced freak power and ragged Confederate ever glory. New wave renegade cool Holden Caulfield disenchantment, big belly, pork-fed interior linemen binge drinking, silent majority Rebel yell ran headlong alongside Beatles, Stones, Steve McQueen wistful neo coolio.

On any given day you could wander into a fraternity house – and find a piss inebriated Kappa Alpha nerd with a topless 'cutting loose' vixen sloppy on his shoulders answering the door. Inside you'd come across Butch Ducharme doing nude pile driver pushups into an equally naked beautiful coed, surrounded by cheering, chanting 'gridiron transfers' who by chance missed getting on the doomed Marshall University Thundering Herd chartered Southern Airways Douglas DC-9 that went down killing all 75 people on board – 37 players, eight coaches, 25 boosters and 5 flight crew – the largest sports related disaster in history. U of R had the survivors and they, like all of us, were living large.

I could quaintly pick up a possum on a wooded way across campus, gently tuck the critter in beside a sleeping sex starved fellow who performed robed 'Black Masses' as a rolling tribute to Marquis de Sade, his scarred face scrubbed raw and red in an effort to eradicate acne … the entire dorm uproariously assembled about the bed like alien dream crashers as both man and beast simultaneously awoke in dilated sensory horror.

Day one we were assailed with 'product packs' of grooming/hygiene crap in an effort by Proctor & Gamble to capture our nubile minds, futilely attempting to enslave our collective and individual purchasing power for a lifetime.

Crest toothpaste, Vitalis – useless slick down hair oil in an age of long flowing male locks … we quickly discovered the alcohol-based liquid made a perfect fire bomb, poured so often beneath doors of fellow students' rooms then set ablaze that all who awoke surrounded by ceiling-high hellfire, simply arose zombie like, beat out the firestorm then returned to bed and deep sleep without even opening the door to see who the arsonist was this time.

Racial disquiet and gender division were non-existent for me.

One of my dearest friends was a black b-ball scholarship point guard student. He called me cracker and I called him nigger with love.

I maintain true love and brotherhood most readily and organically emerge from verbal freedom and trust rather than imposed correctness.

I remember not even being aware of homosexuality until perhaps sophomore year in college – despite the steady gusher of neighborhood jack off masters that had flitted in and out of my life tapestry since the age of six.

Mildly interested in performance, one day I stopped into the fine arts building – peeked through giant oaken doors. Coming as I was from sports gladiatorial show time middle linebacker masculinity, the gender bending theatrical department was like Adam Rippon life forms stepping off a gaudy birthday cake, skittering across the ice sprinkling infectious leprosy spores.

I closed the door quickly - took me a couple of years New York Theater inoculation before I could have reveling affection/fascination/respect for bright, highly talented and sensitive men plucking their facial hair out with clam shells on the way to voluntary castration.

New media and advertising communities are so tremor desperate to architect 'pride & diversity' they crawl the world prowling for Chinese kids born with six toes and prehensile vestigial genitalia to all white divorced Latter-Day Saints polygamous organ harvesters.

Kids of Asian or Black ethnicity appear like spontaneous spores in the midst of all white TV families. Every couple is bi-racial in multitudinous ad.

And why not, the media social foisting running fast and all-consuming might bleed off the identity racial overheating.

*****

Weekends, we went high into the Shenandoah Mountains, car sound systems blazing with early Allman Brothers, (Duane still lived) and every other first time, non-derivative musical act of the day.

It had never happened before! No one had ever generated such sounds! Save founding black fathers Muddy, Sun and Screaming Jay ... Brit aberrant lizards like Link Ray ...

As we neared the campsites, we gobbled LSD.

The structure of tents and *facilities* we 'constructed' suffered for the disorientation and hallucinations, as did boyfriend/girlfriend relationships.

Simple aerodynamics asserted itself; tents became wind tunnels on the mountains and partners shifted with the Electric Kool-Aid Timothy Leary tumult.

My girlfriend at the time was a striking, overtly sexual young woman with a unique origin.

American, born and raised to Christian evangelical ministers serving in Japan, she had morphed by psychological and physiological environment into resembling a Japanese woman. By incredible absorption of her surroundings, her dark almond shaped eyes actually became slanted, her complexion inexplicably turned Nipponese in color.

With our typical accurate laughing lack of sensitivity we anointed her 'The Yellow Overseer'.

Looking back, I wish I had extended more love, wish I had possessed more, externalized more loving chivalry.

Adding to her potential for cultural confusion was her sudden displacement into the pre-feminist paradox of hyper-femininity that many southern women thrashed through.

I recognized the symptoms vividly.

My mother came from the same still bubbling froth, nucleic acid dripping with feminine stereotype.

It's the kind of maelstrom that causes young southern girls to be virgins until one night they decide to get it on with the entire front interior line of the Georgia Bull Dog football team (combined weight 3,300lbs if you factor in the hammer & testicles), next morning reverting to VIP waxed 'delusional virginity' before marrying the dashing heir to the Phillip Morris cig fortune in ceremonial pomp.

As the LSD exploded in our still unfolding brains, high above the Blue Ridge Skyline Drive, as Hendrix's ELECTRIC LADYLAND album revealed all forms of music ever conceived, the Overseer drifted from me to the humor and madness of a friend.

The cock dissonance seemed not to serve her.

When we returned to the university campus, she roamed nude about the Collegiate Gothic buildings, rose before the assembled student body in the Greek amphitheater and renounced the constrained anti - feminine structures of the south, collapsed in breakdown, was carted away sedated in a strait jacket, institutionalized in a psych ward, to emerge months later, safely sequestered in all-women's Roanoke College, preened for ovum matrimony – Dixie Nip woman arc.

The alternative for women was often bitter, smash-mouth alcoholism and denial, Martha Mitchell being the archetype, put down like a wayward jowly pit for laying unrestrained feces along the boulevard. *Too many Nixon state secrets gurgling from the blowsy surly bitch ...*

I took up sculpture, stealing billiard balls as raw material from the student center, scouring junkyards for odd bits of treasure, and then conceiving kinetic whimsical apparatus with 'found' objects.

I discovered the power of history and English, engorged on centuries old periods of human activity, quantities of revolution, endeavor, science, art and war, spewed it back in accelerated exams half crazed with 'White Crosses'… furiously amphetamined, laughably intent on essays, I growled at instructors who tried to gather papers at the end of the designated period.

They backed away.

*****

One hot Monday night just after four students died at Kent State on May 4, 1970 my friends from Connecticut arrived in their converted camper 'milk truck,' first leg of a cross country jaunt. Bunel, Height and Godenzi with his partially blown off hand and shrapnel littered body fresh from Nam.

A Richmond block party was in full swing, an arty 'rainbow coalition' - before Obama the Benedict Arnold even conjured the lie to sell – in the 'Fan' area of the city that had recently 'seceded' from the union and Federalist power.

The fully geared up tactical police with a line of Doberman/Airedale super dogs snarling at the leash sealed both ends of the block. A police car pulled beside me. I had palmed a brick from one of the historical residences. There ten feet from me, like some anti-Rockwell portrait, was the police officer's head framed through the passenger side glass.

I held for a moment, one of those decisive defining seconds … senses sparking like grass fire in concentric rings. Knowing that the brick heave would alter my being forever I held back. Blessed control, fear of capture, and for all the rebellion, a passionate patriot ambivalence … whose side was I truly on? I weaved together with the students as an 'observer,' yes, for all my 'checkering,' Lancelot, Arthur and their goodly light, but part of me, a huge patriot portion lay with the soldiers in Viet Nam.

I felt a calculation of violence, and a simultaneous universal identification with both police and party reveler. This cop sliding by wasn't my enemy, the rag tag bums streaking around hauling North Viet Nam flags weren't my friends.

Allan Ginsberg and his eclectic poetically 'Red' bi-sexual entourage arrived.

A brick from the roof in SLOW-MO, downward, plainly interminably visible, smashed directly into the skull of a suited tac officer.

His body stayed upright for a long second – one thousand, two thousand - the lights already out, held rigid only by the balanced condition of his locked-out knees – then he collapsed, pitch forward to full faced crushing contact with the Boulevard.

Enraged, the tac cops released the half-breed canine monsters, so jacked on savagery a couple bent their bodies double and attacked their handlers ... the pack line shredded their carnivorous path through panicked, stampeding celebrants.

I flew down the street with the horde, Godenzi, a student buddy named Lee moving fast with me in the terror mob. I dashed into an alley. A 15" wall loomed across our escape route.

The beasts turned with us.

Godenzi (despite his missing digits) and I went over with the agility of Olympians; Lee didn't make the cut. He hung on the wall had his right buttock fully carved off by a spit spewing snarling hound.

He was dragged away hemorrhaging to arrest and hospital.

*****

Rare jeweled snow fell one night on the bucolic ornate U. of R. campus. This called for a snowball festival/war by Richmond College 'men'. The cry for a 'panty raid' spilled through the disparate ranks - intense sexual firing on white landscape – the march across the 'lake' to Westhampton Women College, fresh women welcoming the onrushing, smiling 'men', smiling at pewter dorm windows ... a few semen like snowballs smashed against the panes and the feminine faces of eager innocence were transformed before this male rapine insanity. A mob rushed through the corridors filled with terrorized cute co-eds, some bloody cut by flying glass a mere moment after their coaxing affection.

A weird time in a weird world. Sparkles from the Acid sky, the power of panties, Viet Nam, 'revolution' – youth energy, rampant new, I could meet a beauty from Italy, Brazil or Spain on the sidewalk and be sleeping with her twenty minutes later - "You pazzo boy!" "Voce e louco!" "Estas loco!"

Glimpses – great swathes of terror of the Left revealed – spitting on troops (decades of psychological debilitation results) *romanticized bombings and bank robberies, cop killings New York to LA.*

Another night, at a Janis Joplin concert, so close her sweat flinging onto us, the enflamed Yippie fools stormed the President's residence at the University of Virginia, howling for the torching destruction of a structure conceived and constructed by Thomas Jefferson himself.

At that they lost me, became enemies of liberty.

The President of the University emerged from the front door at midnight, perfectly groomed, three-piece suit and watch fob. His presence washed over the fools, their infantile rage dissipated by his calm courage. "Go home", he said and as the challenged children they were, they did just as the father commanded.

It was a faux Playland Party revolt ...

Up in D. C., I watched bent Students for a Democratic Society (SDS) surge toward the Justice Department.

Throughout the District kids donned gas masks, built barricades by turning over parked cars, battled the armored 'turtle' - fully geared-up tactical police packing tear gas shotguns and hard skull cracking shafts.

I gazed over seas of students clamoring over the stirring architectural legacy of Washington, snipers poised on roofs and yellow school buses ringed Nixon's White House in defense.

I remember thinking, "My God they're going to bring the government down"

Wrong perception.

I watched as a single horse policeman became separated from his unit across the green grass bridge, where now the sunken WWII Memorial resides.

A demonstrator, a large black man, refused to move along as the mounted cop used his horse to drive the man away. The horse was trained to high step against mobs.

The black man turned, and with all his shoulders/back behind the blow, punched the horse in the chest in rage, clear animal cruelty.

Unflinching the horse continued to high-step, pressing the fellow backward. The demonstrator turned and ground his lit cigarette out in the chest of the horse.

The cop went wild, swinging his baton at the thug.

The mob of baked revelers, hippies, college age partiers, quasi kitchen 'revolutionaries' surged forward and pulled the cop from his horse.

Wrong move.

Across the grassy bridge, between silver isthmus pools filled with naked and stoned, the full company phalanx of mounted police wheeled and charged, a full plunging gallop in zenith equestrian power.

I watched transfixed, sensing and knowing history was in the making, heavy cavalry against infantry experientially. (Much later, BRAVEHEART got it right cinematically, don't ya know.) The demonstrators had no large tree lances to blunt and repel the onslaught. The cavalry played swift and skilled polo with their skulls and faces.

*****

The government held of course, because at heart, the majority of demonstrators were dilettantes, just as actors today are political dilettantes.

Does revolution have value if it would burn buildings of mythology, disrupt the innocent, trash the hood, even tear up the freedom symbols inspiring allied troops and people throughout the centuries and the world?

Their 'Revolution', indulged and entitled, largely anti-intellectual and bratty, incubated with Mao and marbled with hedonism - rather than birthed from sacrifice and enlightenment as was the original American Revolution - little to do with liberty and justice, less chance of survival.

There were true warriors, martyrs of liberation, in the civil rights movement and with the heroes who served in Viet Nam – but not those on either the streets of Washington, nor those who fled to Canada, nor those who piddle about totalitarian tinsel town today.

Still these political, ideological, behavioral strains permeate California and Hollywood.

"I am a nasty woman!" pukes Ashley. Fine memorization Ashley. "I've thought a lot about blowing up the White House," mews Madonna. Attempting not only to cause the rightful depose of power pigs like Harvey Weinstein et al but to topple a rightfully elected President – whose balancing triumphs thus far have brought America back from a legacy – Bill, Gore, Hillary Obama - of treason, mismanagement, global crime, appeasement, retreat from the world.

One marvels at the fraud of righteous cool spoken 21ˢᵗ century suffragette words of poet Nina Donavan being wed to fallen Hillary Clinton, a delusional woman subverting women's and LBGT rights personally by voracious attacks on harassment and rape victims of Bill and geo political alliance via bribes with Saudi Arabia. Clearly the criminal Clinton Foundation and double-dealing of the DNC cock blocking Bernie plays little in the Dem hall monitor harpies of Hollywood.

*****

I am a #metoo victim. Landing from Charles de Gaulle Airport in Paris, spun out by work and jet lag, arrival for the film NIGHT WALK – in Casablanca's Val d'Anfa Hotel. Spectacularly scaled and colorfully adorned, porters with Fez caps, the hotel is perfect for a writer actor hungry for a couple of days before the filmic fray. I dive to the services of the spa, no luxury spared at these frugal prices.

In complete elegant civilization, I am asked to shower, made to sit in herbed vapors.

The lights dim. A 22-year-old massage therapist in nun like white uniform begins the oiled effleurage, kneading my weary jet lagged muscles. I fall as deeply asleep as a Bill Cosby victim.

I awake ...

Her head has descended, and her mouth is on my cock to the hilt. Whoa, Sally come home! I bolt upright and she's buck naked!!!!! Body caramel round silken shapes, panties incongruously still around her ankles in potato sack race mimicry.

I know how these predators function, a condom in her pursed lips to groom me and my member for exploitation.

Laughing I sit up, this is after all my game! Gently I kiss her neck, my fingers find her clit and dance a minuet.

She rears backward, brown nipples and perfect breasts rising as she pants. She and I form a pirouetting multiped twirling and crashing about the space, the whore furiously pumps my hardening penis with her grip, my digit doing Keith Moon in her money-maker, sensuous probing to manic wet plunge.

She attempts speech, but the condom garbles her French Arabic. I grin even in my moment of 'shame and degradation', skills reasserting despite four years relationship bliss (later!

As she sinks toward the floor cumming, shudders out only ... "1,000!" meaning the local 10 to 1 currency, about $100.

I laughed, separated my fingers from vulva ... "Il ne pas necessaire". It's not necessary!

Both of us could not stray from our precepts, (she money for sex, I Eros equality, women wish to fuck, ejaculate, do the toss and turn irrespective of economics – that bestial gentleness and animal sexuality chivalry coupled with play rapine force ... Might for Sophisticated Brute Right ... is all our balletic sexual birthright.

I bring to the last sacred supper of love something other than cash.

All this in just 15 seconds, the same length of time I had 'dueled' with drunken Michael Madsen over his wife at the Egyptian Theater, premiere for one of his straight to VOD flicks.

My hesitancy had to do with equal parts fidelity and professional integrity. I just didn't want to dissipate my chi energy from filming NIGHTWALK as a towering wounded warrior drug addicted anti-Islamic vessel of hate prison guard (not a stretch) nor waste a million little Patricks on anyone other than my Lady Mia.

Thus far this Muslim majority country seems about as secular as it cums, pun intended.

Still so spectacular is my Stockholm Syndrome with my harasser, I tipped her well and gave her the beautiful pear I had lifted from the breakfast buffet.

I rushed to idiotically share the interlude via phone with Mia and she laughs (brittle), then goes headlong into a caffeine fueled twenty-minute conniption over the possibility of me kissing lips that had sucked a thousand old European distasteful dicks.

"How would you like it if I suddenly sat up and started stroking some massage dude's dick!"

And so NIGHTWALK begins by bringing me face to face with my own marred double standard morality.

NIGHTWALK incidentally will also bring me full body ass cheek soul spiritual anus probe – we are in a cinema prison after all - with Oliver Stone's son Sean.

Tall, French fluent and sophisticated, Sean is playing the western journalist in this Romeo & Juliet fable (my global sales distribution pitch) ... the Eastern Islam Beauty played by Sarah Alami. Eric Roberts will do one of his all too frequent cue card appearances fresh from a VANITY FAIR piece legitimizing his indiscriminate work choices, Richard Tyson will transform himself into an impotent extra with his dissipated turn. I'll have a scene or two with nice, lightweight Louis Mandylor. Tiny Lister - unable to learn lines as well and under Federal indictment - will get himself expelled from the cast.

Mickey Rourke arrives the last day of filming ... a hybrid testament to Darwin through the filthy halls of excess – pancake makeup an inch thick, 12 pack abs and skunk bear mullet.

*****

And just like the 'revolution' of the sixties folded after the Kent State volley which killed four, one has to ask how long will present day U.C. Berkley ANTIFA continue trashing buildings and terrorizing speakers when the one distinguished southern gentleman with real courage meets their juvenility like U. of VA's president faced down the Yippies, when one Martin Luther King with moral force addresses their despotic poison ... or a single volley of rubber bullets tears into them, or perhaps the full jacketed hell of police weaponry truly unleashed.

Not long – they and Hollywood currently exist in scrambled brain and protected false mob bully bravery ... ANTIFA because of SF police/U. of Berkley indulgence and lack of parental supervision ... Tinsel Town wallowing in the safety of pack Liberalism.

The way of youth, often prophetic yet misguided - to attempt to be part of something galvanizing and boldly new.

Liars to the left of me, jokers on the right.

Let us move to our better selves. For that is the purpose of art and existence. That is the soul and seed of our American and human endeavor.

Youth – so eager to say, I *must* be part of something that is against the MAN rightly or wrongly, with thought or without, setting forth into 'new' 'my own' realms of 'liberation' even if it holds little historical relevancy or real world common sense. So what if it aligns with Left or Right reigns of Orwellian failure from fundamental Islam to Scientology to Taliban to Communism (Chinese & otherwise), ANTIFA Nazis to Putin admiration … all through murderous well-meaning compassion and unbalance.

*****

By the James River, on the fringe of Richmond, I ambled tripping with my scarlet haired freckled girlfriend, soon to be *extremely* short-time (7 months) wife #1 *(alluring red haired Catholic daughter of once Police Commissioner of NYC weds immature/boundless Protestant Eros outlaw - last time I didn't listen to my inner murmur "No! You shouldn't marry anyone!")*.

Existential menace rolling down the river of life & the 1st of three fractured marriages finds genesis here …

A car loaded with shitheads rolled by, pig shouts as they pulled over. Exiting the car, a formation of 5 crackers approached along the dirt road that hung above the river.

"Have you seen my doggy? He's a little bitty thing with a pug nose … just like you," snarled the lead cretin. And with that he began what to me in my crystalline hallucinatory state was an incredibly slow and filmic sucker punch. The blow took a millennium to reach my face, glancing off without any real power.

"What's going on?" Said my reinforcement – a classmate named Brock, first person granted conscientious objector status in the history of that region of Virginia. Definitely not a 'Street Fighting Man' by skill set.

They cold cocked him, for a second I was ignored, and in that moment, I had to do something to save myself and the woman, *my woman,* they moved toward to rape.

I hammered my fist into the thug who had hit me. He went down. Two others went low to tackle me. We rolled, crashing down the bank, plunging into the river.

I'm alive in water, the LSD vanishing in an instant, I begin strangling them.

They go limp, drowning, "Oh Christ, I kill these fucking rednecks and I'll have to fill out reams of paperwork!"

I dragged them from the water, pulled them both ashore, sagged exhausted myself, the drug reasserting itself, trees above me between a gulping sky and vibrating earth.

Another of the gang loomed over me, raised a heavy branch club high to crush my head.

One of the two gasping on the ground raised his hand, hoarsely, "No, he saved us!"

Then they rose up and all ran away into the car, gunned away, stalled and stuck the vehicle in the soil trying to turn around. They fled into the forest.

Cops arrived, summoned by my girl who had run to a near cabin. The weird mind fuck atrocity was the cops looked exactly like the assailants, *florid fleshy undulating faces,* jovial at the prospect of writing up just another dust up in the wilderness.

I was on full alert 24/7 for two years.

As I entered any room, hallway, club, any arbitrary space my senses were enflamed and extended, roving for attackers. Imagine the true victim of any dismemberment, rape, war, or genocide.

Exhausting …

Seventeen: Anemia & Bandages, Law Comes as Hairy Men with Shotguns

"Come on in here Ranger! I'll make that dream come true!" Lyle Gutherie / WALKER, TEXAS RANGER

Events of violent proboscis damage *(broken noses, splintered nostrils – mine)* marched on as did my mode of relationships involving disrupted adultery (mine), broken heart couplings, indiscriminant single encounters, sex anywhere, anytime, any female of every class, education or IQ, delightful unrestricted seizure of the titillated moment.

I had crushed my nose five more times as a teenager - once a year.

I broke my nose once fighting in the street, once collegiate wrestling, another time when a magnificent horse named Rebel reared and flung his head backward, once in football when a friend named Jim Fecto charged over my face. I still bear the chin scars from his spikes.

It was decided by my parents that I should have corrective nasal surgery once more under my father's insurance before I exited college.

It was arranged to happen during Thanksgiving break in Virginia Beach under the over watch of my father's lifelong friend Judge Reed Spencer and his wife.

The night before the surgery, my mother's Holy Roller sister, Aunt Louise came bedside with her daughter. My aunt insisted she had to pray over me in case I passed away the following morning. As she mumbled scripture I zeroed

189

in on my cousin who was setting my kindling ablaze. Divergent whims zinged about the room.

Procedure performed, five days later I left hospital, returned to my Freckle One's white flesh, her contemporary appointed, tastefully decorated digs, began to frolic fuck with her.

My nose began to bleed, onrushing towel sopping fill the abattoir gutter bleeding. I was taken to the hospital, once more covering the inside of a vehicle with red splatter.

18 hours later … after two transfusions, the doctor leaping over my inert body on the table, stabbing my chest with 2 adrenaline loaded back from the dead heart PULP FICTION dagger length needles – they were able to stop the blood from pouring down the ruptured rear nasal cavities, cascading down my throat, pooling toxically in my stomach, causing me to violently vomit, tearing the surgical nose wounds even wider.

Exploding in bed makes for strange but authentic courtships – years later both my elbows burst while making love to my 3rd wife, splashing the scene with brownish bursitis fluid. Ladies, you know a man is special when he sacrifices body parts and blood cells for love as you're wrapping your thighs around him. The women in my life have always taken such bio disruption in stride.

Two weeks later after members of the family from far flung Eastern America came and paid bedside vigil to the anemic near death son, I left the hospital, head, face swathed in bandages, frail, suffering brain migraines from lack of red blood cells.

I stumbled into the house I shared with two other students, sat quietly at the table for a single moment - exams tomorrow – and bearded plain clothes shot-gun wielding Richmond narcs ruptured thru windows and doors with sledge hammers.

One roommate had sold something to an undercover narc somewhere in Richmond.

Freckled One, her best friend Laura, two friends from California – a couple who'd opted to visit in my room as I had surgery - my two housemates and myself were all jailed for felonies amidst broken glass, wood splinters and winter Richmond air – admittedly mild – wafting through gaping holes in the domicile.

Felony LSD (two tablets in one roomie's locked box, the aforementioned seller), felony speed (2 tabs same box), misdemeanor marijuana (2 seeds vacuumed from the *flung together carpet remnant floor). The heavy charges heaped on in the usual play to squeeze guilty pleas on the lesser charges.*

I found myself sitting in a cell, head swathed in bandages like the Man in the Iron Mask until my God Mother Jean, my mother's college mate and lifelong frenemy, sweetly bailed me out so I could continue to reverentially sneak around the back of her house to watch her shower her Botticelli body.

$2400 dollars in legal fees later – dismissed.

This blood drained last waning days collegiate was placed on Disciplinary Probation by Richmond College - 'presumption of innocence till found guilty' a flowing, often ignored concept and in my young manhood probably not something to extend to me in any case – not in head rush days of '72.

Two booked roommates?

One – an innocent as well - became one of the world's first and greatest male models, widely celebrated. Last time I saw him he was soothing medicated salve onto his tool in the kitchen as I ushered a truly beautiful British girl into our Antebellum residence after a protracted period of persuasion to allay her fears of the 'House of the Rising Sun' in which I resided.

Brit girl fled – visons of genital warts, syphilis, gonorrheal contagion swimming in her head - our love never to be consummated.

As we all went out the door in cuffs, the other housemate, Black Irish John Oates – *it had been his locked box* – swore he would assume full rap for his drugs. Course he didn't – wouldn't expect him to.

You could get less time in Richmond for mounting your barn animal *and a same sex nephew in the public square on the Sabbath than for an oz. of weed.*

They would have publicly stuffed his anus with Arby's over a pep rally bonfire spit – the T.C. Williams School of

Law ceremony pitched together by cops from Hampton Roads to the Smithfield Ham factory.

John cleared jail, 6 months later soared his car off a cliff in doomed vivaciousness, broke his neck, and died 6 months after that from complications due to paralysis

Eighteen: City Young Man

"Even if we do, how do we know it's not already too late for us?" Red One / DARK ANGEL

During university breaks I worked as dishwasher, truck driver, factory hand, swimming, rowing, tennis sailing camp counselor at a remarkable place on Cape Cod.

Pleasant Bay was a huge basin opening to the larger Atlantic with a shallow depth of no more than 4-5 feet. The only boats that could navigate the shallows had retractable rudders.

We – campers and counselors alike - would cast ourselves nude overboard to troll on long lines trailing behind the camp sailing craft. Leagues and hours of being pulled swiftly through soft aqua plant rushes caressing the lengths of our bodies, half fish, half Aqua Surfer.

I had a brief career in construction (days), in concrete pouring (two weeks), waiting tables at the Richmond Howard Johnsons (months).

The hostess and I were the only whites.

I quickly was labeled 'Eater', when I expressed a fondness for pussy lapping, an activity running counter to the black kitchen staffs' hygienic and cultural bias.

Revulsion for my gash relish was also cover for jealously at my education. One of them drew a knife down on me. We fought inconclusively until those blacks who liked both of us intervened.

I said goodbye to pouring cascading cement, sludge streaming the trough, pebbles, small nuggets shooting to within the inner lining of my boots, shredding calf and shin flesh as I furiously rushed before the hardening setup … carving flesh at night with the 29-year-old restaurant hostess.

"I have five thousand dollars, stay with me," she offered. God love her, bids for me were rising but no …

I graduated from tranquil Richmond College, And despite her clenching legs and welcoming spirit, left Richmond as young people have before, Lee, Stuart and Stonewall still on Monument Avenue - *how the virulent white supremacists of 2017 have perhaps screwed the pooch on that one now* – left concerts of Ike and Tina Turner, Iron Butterfly, Blood Sweat and Tears, Chicago, Springsteen (the 'Boss' in early groups Mercy Flight and Steel Mill), the liberal arts serenity and secular Baptist overtones.

I had drawn number 364 - my birthday August 20th - in the Military Draft Lottery. They never got above 200.

You exit school and wonder where destiny lies. I said, I'll go for the light show, bomb runs, strafing, cooking off ordinance, aerial glamor. I passed the Navy Flight initial physical.

They hadn't caught my broken back or asthma.

Flight you had to sign for six years. Military friends took me aside, told me the Navy would spot the back/breathing issues, wash me out. You then had to stay a sailor for the six. I fanned out the papers on my bed – recommendations, transcripts … there for the signing. Roll the dice.

No thank you, not if I didn't have good certainty of flying.

I headed to New York City, following that redhead.

She'd graduated and departed a year early which of course explains the how I might raid the hostess, this girl named something, that ginger named something else … a brunette called – whatever – the squadrons of females I might board, sack and abandon drifting in a sea of flotsam.

I'm not saying I was the only pirate. There were females of peek and pillage, scoot in for a round of provisions at the gunwale, slip a line and be gone – many more offering heart and allegiance. I just wasn't a fit man.

Part unconscious – incessant movement, sheer collection and compartmentalization, hot to trot experiment – part the age, it was the sixties and seventies.

There was dishonesty to it. Have your cake … eat the bakery too. Always a central girl, main squeeze … waiting somewhere, several disseminated like ports of light and emotion.

I was always exceedingly grateful … for each individual splayed fortune placed beneath my Christmas tree …

The odd thing – being with one increased the ardor for the other and vice versa. A pinball machine of desire and experience … and oh, how adept at diving for the seduction

196

I was – find the hole in the line and this *offensive* end would and could go for the light.

As I stabbed Richmond's pussys – head down, collide at the gap, romping untethered, hurting hearts, breaking trusts … Miss Freckles Catholic of Manhasset, Long Island *in the company of her mother* plans our elaborate feast of hundreds wedding.

*****

As a premier act in New York, I was asked to join a crew serving as bodyguards/security for rock groups. The crew was largely New York Jets in off-season - big boys.

One of the bodyguards was an early prototypical body builder stage named Adonis. He gave out cards that said, "Worship Adonis". He and I were the smallest among the giants.

So in my early twenties, well before I became an actor, I was one of Jimi Hendrix's bodyguards … not in London when he died, but whenever he appeared in New York City or nearby Long Island or New Jersey. I saw him so many times I became bored, even when he was, of course, intrinsically mind-blowing. I cut loose doing security for Jethro Tull, The Grateful Dead (I preferred Quicksilver Messenger Service, the Dead's front band and jam bandit mates), Procol Harum, The Beach Boys.

I beat up Dennis Wilson one night which is not saying much. He was certainly high, a low motor skills opponent trotting while disturbed. I worked for Jeff Beck, Jefferson

Airplane, Rod Stewart, Steve Marriott/Humble Pie, Pink Floyd, etc. ... free form drug substances, micro biology inspired kaleidoscope light shows, raucous, sweet, mad anarchic 'festival' seating and of course *the music, the sounds, reverb, wah-wah, clarion notes, anthems, machine gun scales, vocal growls and operatic audio kites trailing away and suspended in the firmament.*

As a child, I played recorder in a school fife and drum corps, participated in heady local parades passing through picturesque Connecticut villages. To this day, I can play all the hymns of the various branches of the military. When I began body guarding, I carried a large, hard plastic alto recorder to while away idle moments and to use as a Billy club.

I had already learned a great deal about the nature of mobs during this time. A mob is a coward. As they threw bottles at us, cursed us in alcohol and drugged fueled stupor, I learned to choose one, a single fucking culprit in the center of the crap wave and then attack. Wade into the swill and beat that one senseless, without mercy, swiftly. The mob will run, terrified before the solo fearless assault.

One night in the Bronx, while Beck and Rod Stewart belted and cut a caper on stage, amidst crumbling steel decay, apocalypse before apocalypse, there was a mob in motion suddenly at one of the park's entry points, sensed more than actually seen. I went over twirling the recorder.

A bodyguard's face had been freshly carved up with what must have been a large, surgically sharp blade. From hairline, across the ear, scything down moon shaped through the cheek to lip's edge, open, pulsating pink like a pussy in fresh orgasm, a flesh ocean shell ripe from violence.

He seemed in shock, mumbling, "They went down there", pointing to the underworld beneath the elevated subway – a ripped landscape of pulverized metropolis, layers of crunching black gravel, a dark opera of disjointed structure above, sparse steel pillars.

A cadre of bodyguards came together as wolves, streamed downward into the blue nether of the broken city, a panorama of k-bar wreckage and baseball size concrete lumpen. The bodyguard family sailed into the industrial pillage with purpose.

There ahead – the guilty, three tall sleek forms, utterly leather clad, from boot to high collared jacket, a woman and two men, each with black scapula length hair.

"I'm Losing You" pulsed from above, narrowing and honing of our collective nervous system began occurring. Animal war, senses quickening, adrenaline through blood.

Big cats, lions, tigers, surge forward with constricting field 'tunnel vision'. Why? Because they have so few predators they don't fear flank strikes. The sides aren't a source of danger. Wolves, as we were, war as a pack, and must possess surround vision and focused striking capability, allowing coordination with each other, lunge and parry of attack without wounding allies.

Where was that huge blade that had carved up my brother bodyguard's face? I knew it was there in their clothing, hidden, waiting to be revealed I was sensible enough not to want to be on the receiving end of its lethal point.

Who isn't wary of long knives, machetes, axes and shotguns. The wounds so catastrophic - hunting and living on the farm had seared this into me as a child. Self-safety (*common sense for Christ sake*) caused me to circle the prey.

My bodyguard brothers held no hesitation or flanking instinct. I was stunned as they swarmed the three in an instant, like tearing leopards: fearless, they took their prey down, over-running, swarming to kill the males.

The woman was screaming at crystal cracking decibels. From within the slaughter, one of the leather clad men bravely stood up with the large knife, almost sword like, giving off light between his legs, and cried out in a clarion voice – "Leave that man alone!" The pack fell away, backward to a distance of 10-15 feet.

The knife man bent to gather his brother, pulled him to his feet for a second of erect height, just as a first piece of concrete, thrown by Adonis, hit him in the chest full force. The wolves had each picked up concrete balls and full-arm heaved them methodically at the standing pair, stoning them slowly in a medieval ceremony.

The pair stood there inert as the concrete meteors smashed their faces, their hands, blade falling useless, both sinking to their knees, teeth crushed, jaws and skulls bloody, smashed and misshapen.

The woman continued to shriek across the subterranean city debris. Police eventually came and gathered the remains. We returned to stand gently to the side under the sky cityscape, gray with intensely beautiful hues, listening to the show. Rod Stewart had progressed to "Maggie May".

This was really just the beginning of the change from fun and love to the descent to increasing violence.

People screaming on acid bolted through giant coliseum windows, leaving Pompeii-like human-shaped shadow gaps in the plate glass, Keith Haring road runner figures captured by the helter-skelter of their hallucinations. They would be run down by the authorities a mile or two down the road, speckled with blood and glass.

I saw a young man shot gunned to death. The police returned, the children of love under the influence proved incapable of self-rule.

I left the rock body-guarding when killings, shootings, stabbings - obscene and pervasive – became commonplace.

It was never meant to be a career, but a time when police were not desired beings at musical venues and a young man with an alto recorder could wade the arcade frontier, watching details of funhouse civilization.

Nineteen: Magazine Maypole, Isle of Tremulous Tongue, Le Mort De Perry Ellis

"I know who you are. I know all your secrets. I know the dark places you hide. I know what you do when you are alone. I know your dreams. It's time to share your dreams." Byron Volpe / PARASOMNIA

New York City in the seventies was as John Lennon pronounced 'Rome', center of the civilized empire, and so what then was 50 Rockefeller Center – home of TIME, INC. - where I landed and worked, cruising in with an Oregon firefighter's suit and Nikes amongst pinstriped Yalies and Harvard graduates?

Ground Zero of the thumping heart of the empire, media and otherwise. I was at the CENTER. greatest magazine and publishing fiefdoms in the world.

Starting with the crown jewel LIFE Magazine, to be one of the pivotal team launching the iconic publication again as a monthly…TIME, FORTUNE, PEOPLE, SPORTS ILLUSTRATED, COSMOPOLITAN, CYCLING, BOATING, MODERN BRIDE, POPULAR PHOTOGRAPHY, POPULAR MECHANICS, PSYCHOLOGY TODAY, LUXE, THE NEW YORK TIMES … preeminent pictorial & textural journals.

HBO was a closet down the hall where geeks wanked. The magazines reigned, and we were the creative princelings.

How sad so many once omnipotent news sources have fallen into few page, few viewer decay as they assembled among the rampantly biased anti-Trump, spasming in congenital and tribal delusion as they seek a 'Dan Ratheresque' Watergate moment.

"Let me, let me cry out truth to power!!!!!!!!!!!!" I'm a reporter too!!! I can rip Trump just as Dan ripped Dick Nixon!!!! ... shucking journalistic integrity with the fevered urgency of an adult attempting to duplicate an 11-year old's 1st shower ejaculation.

Auto asphyxia 'journalism' – "I can't get a fame hard on by pursuing Hillary, Bill, Gore – that would betray my Left 'Ho Chi Minh' root system. I'd rather hang myself on a doorknob of bias and bullshit, somehow I'll tweak out a wiener".

Stricken with untruth, spin, fakery, political delusion that our moment in time is the black information equivalent of the plague that ravaged the 14th century, destroying credibility of church and state, giving rise to 'modern reasoning existential man' - humankind seeks candor and authenticity just as much of media shamelessly fails in fulfillment of its truth and moral patriotic delivery.

There is an axiom of advertising and magazine publishing – "Convince them you're a genius in the first month, then you can coast for two years" ... not me, I was born from the womb with accelerant drive!

Glory to be paid to create, beginning as Hunter Thompson, Oliver Stone, other leopards had ... ushered by Eugene

Smith's iconic pictures, the founding 'reportage' photography of Alfred Eisenstaedt and Andre Kertesz …

Oh lucky man! To possess the exceptional experience of literate work, to create intelligently, causing people to take their hand, slide it in their pocket and send money to the dream conveyed by ads and journalism with empathy and insight into their aspirations.

The skill set of advertising and journalism is remarkably conjoined to acting, a similar twin, self-placement within the 'others' dreams and hungers.

Nine to five, copywriting layouts and magazine articles, picking up literal writing cadence, rhythms and structures, scintillating, hyper authentic leads and cyclical gliding ends, embraced and surrounded by other young men and women … eating steaks, lobster, the birth of sushi on a little conveyor belt eatery on 34th Street … fucking on graphic arts tables with lithe visual artists from anywhere exotic, love among agencies and media titans …

… rock body guarding at night, paid with 50 tickets per show, scalping, everyone running gate and security breaches for high, illicit dollars. Hells Angels crating off a statue of David in the Academy of Music (pretty, this belongs in our clubhouse – have at it fellows), stabbings, shotguns and knives taking weak sheep from the herd, the greatest musical arrivals and departures in the history of the world were blossoming everywhere.

Dawn, lay down, smoke some Angel Dust and go through tie-dye canvases stretched and framed in this or that loft space and arrive at Jupiter.

Weekends making love with blonds from California, Florida and Montana, each crying out "ooooooooh" when they came or when they clung to me cruising the Moto Guzzi 850, a 'Rich Man's Bike' whipping from its parking spot beside somebody's Rolls … out to the splashing color palette of New England, up as far as the primordial ancient Maine forests and post card perfect Stratton, Vermont snow - the run from NYC geographical severing: breaking ice, leaping in the stream after skiing all day and sauna love making, delicious meals and mind altering madness, couples exchanging partners amidst fresh illegal substances and oxygen, nude snow adultery impressions on long wood walks and finally an energized melancholy road back to the City, night sky blue to Monday morning magazine work once again.

… or as close as eastward beaches, swimming, sunbathing Fire Island, the Hamptons, your girl's tits making the beach tantalized and nervous … to conclaves of rugger madmen binge alcoholics, All-Metro Union, Old Maroon and Old Blue – Bronx and Manhattan brotherhood of booze and bruises.

My body was now fully resurrected from the car accident … back into athletic wars. There are plenty of places on a rugby pitch for one groomed in American football and spear tackling, you become brilliant or injured swiftly in ten-yard bursts of thigh power.

When I played the Aspen Annual Rugger Fest, the halftime entertainment was two young men injured the previous year with broken necks, rehabilitated for months. Now they were set to stand from their wheelchairs unaided. They nearly made it before brother hands had to intervene and help.

*****

BLUEBOY, an early mag repository for Warhol output, gay artists and wandering yours truly, bought a celebratory ode article to rugby camaraderie from me.

As I was transfixed by genial violence, abandon and athleticism – *male and female*, yes, there are, astonishing female rugby teams - so too BLUEBOY was eager for man on man down and dirty field of dreams pieces.

My devotion to the disciplined, athletic female form – with plenty of wide latitude for curvy, rail thin, upside, down side, who cares as long as it's female and sexy spirit is in the form, desire comes in all shapes and sizes and colors – had its beginnings in women equestrians, these lady ruggers and then powerfully to the mono mind disciplined virginal acolytes of ballet.

I culled only those too tall and large breasted for long term careers in ballet. Those that would soon bolster modern dancer ranks ... where diversity of form was more beautifully malignant.

BLUEBOY saw what they saw, exalted in my homage to brotherhood in the homo ambiance of the scrum – tight shorts and mystique of the 'virgin hetero' as yet unsullied by cock.

One day I noted their 'Man of the Year Contest'. $10,000 to the winner.

I was in great shape, flew to Nassau in the Bahamas, got a bit golden and sea scrubbed, charmed a woman on the beach, placed a camera in her hands, stepped out of my bathing suit against waves crashing mussel clotted cliffs.

Submitted the pics …

Barry McKinley, a top international photographer raving safari gay man was assigned by the mag, quick enough I was anointed a centerfold, complete with fluffed cock and elegant tux.

I met Robert Hayes, managing editor of INTERVIEW at the shoot, began doing assignments for Warhol and his mag … really novel being the only 'straight' creature cavorting on a gay planet.

The pictures also sold to 'closeted' PLAYGIRL. John C. Reilley, brilliantly lampoons this confession in STEPBROTHERS.

I picked up a 17-year old virgin ballerina at Lincoln Center; outside Café Des Artistes – most impeccable thin crust gourmand pizza in the world - the texture of her body – she had difficulty, bustier and taller than most dancers, she became my dancer lover for seven years in and out, while she became mistress of iconic actor James Coburn.

She would return to me periodically in New York as
Coburn aged in LA. A decade later I had the gift of
working with Coburn - an elegant man if ever one existed -
in GREYHOUNDS.

He told me of his arthritis agonies from early alcohol – like
a boy delighted by Christmas morning discoveries - his
hands knotted, knuckles medieval, pain and misshapen
forms alleviated by vigorous massage, brutal manipulations
- *get rid of those troublesome gout crystals by blood flow.*

I told the ballerina I couldn't betray Coburn anymore. I
admired him too much.

Coburn and his lady produced the women centric Arthurian
mini-series AVALON together, then separated. Just before
he died I glimpsed him at Spago with a clearly adoring,
richly beautiful woman. He did alright.

A year or so ago, I was in a Montana Avenue ice cream
shop. A tap on my shoulder.

"Patrick."

I turned, there was a old, frumpy, frizzy haired rotund
woman. Unrecognizable.

"It's Lisa ..." I was stunned, ballerina gone south.

"This is my husband. Dr. –." She gestured behind her to a
nebbish, clearly uncomfortable figure.

I was so shocked by the degrading, so dismayed by the fall
– *the abandonment lack of discipline* - I flashed angry,
quickly, even rudely, turned away.

I so regret my gracelessness. I should have taken her in my
arms, whispered how beautiful she was and told her how
much she meant to me.

*****

So many beautiful women flitting through New York at
TIME, INC and elsewhere, never really lingering,
entwining with brief rapture, each making their own
orgasmic song, an intricacy of individuality, energy, lips,
legs, the shifting, vectoring wives of philandering friends,
twinkling brunette editors, executive lady VP's rising from
PLAYBOY ranks as Hugh Hefner battled Bob Guccionne
& Penthouse.

*All around – me & thee – sex - art directors, delicate
secretaries, editors, Asian graphic designers spread upon
desks (how marvelous I was a man in an age when
company-wide couplings were encouraged, hailed as
performance incentives), models, snow bunnies, ballerinas,
Puerto Rican maids, cops, Christian girl – still calls -
evangelical Studio 54 wistful post mescaline sponge baths,
Le Jardin she-creatures hungry - eat each other,
Mineshaft/Anvil urine fountain tubs & chain link ass
expulsion acts, Continental Baths, Fire Island, Hamptons
sand sex angels, Justin Trudeau's trucker fuck mom, Jacob
Javits' trucker fuck wife - Plato's Retreat laughing at*

sullen bulbous grotesque slime ... sleepless TIME boy gone social – grateful, always & forever.

I sat on the high steps of my 73rd street brown stone between Central Park West and Columbus and watched Carly Simon stride by, legs beginning at her neck, lips unfolding in large enticing allure.

"May I buy you an organic orange juice?"

"I have orange juice at home. Why don't you come with me to have some?"

My confidence is substantial, but I was momentarily blown away.

"Don't you have 'security' issues?"

"You have honest eyes."

I pretended I didn't know who she was. Instinctively I knew that would preserve the attraction, be the manure for love to grow.

"What's your name?'

"Patrick. And you?"

"Carly ..." She hung on my response ... waiting.

I gave my best questioning grey eyed wolf vapid incomprehensible dead in space stare.

"What?"

Away we went to her residence, the rarefied Dakota penthouse. A frail dissipated (heroin) James Taylor peeked in the door to drop off the children. Michael Caine called, making arrangements to go to Jamaica with the ease we mortals use for pop over to CVS. A pure snow-white grand piano was poised over the view of the Park through floor to ceiling windows.

I sipped my organic OJ.

The visit moved to conclusion. I knew we were poised for further ascension, *I could feel it in me fingers, feel it in me toes (and elsewhere)* - God only knows what that one was capable of spinning. She moved close to me at the door, eyes and lips inches from mine, she smiled, I blurted the truth – such would be the foundation for mushrooming intimacy!

"I know who you are."

Her eyes went cold, Michael Corleone, catching Diane Keaton in the house after the abortion.

Slowly she closed the door.

*****

I created kismet with a wild Bolivian at a stoplight on Park Avenue. Her car was Ian Flemmingesque – all European smooth form and design - her skin tawny, coal eyes and features sculptural with curvaceous torso over long strong inviting legs.

Leyna looked like a dark haired Brazilian sculpture about to be placed on the prow of a carved aboriginal war canoe. I was similarly tan, just back from a bit of Saint Barthelme in the Caribbean. Live in New York City you learn to get out at least twice a year or the industrial colossus machine will consume you.

A struck-up conversation and a dalliance … she accompanied me to events, all my friends wanted to fuck her.

My hands found Leyna's thighs; she had massive scarring on the landscape leading to her pussy. Her most intimate plumbing always out-of-bounds, she murmured vague inferences about female issues as we kissed.

"When I was I child of twelve," Leyna said. "I fell into a swift river and piranha collided with my legs. I was rescued, and the entire poor village blended their minimal funds and sent me here in New York for surgery. I lived in a volunteer firehouse as I endured many operations."

Between taking her long tongue in my mouth and suckling I was awash in sympathy for her.

*****

Our unrequited affair progressed. Leyna invited me to the island for a weekend. Not Fire Island, a sandbar really, a tiny space the size of a small baseball diamond deposited by millennial waves in Long Island Sound.

She drove at high speed along the Long Island Freeway, whipped into a miniscule boat landing, exited the car with assassin quickness, hit the trunk and withdrew a package. A button hit and gear self-morphed into a fully operational Zodiac racing craft.

I was awed by Leyna's expertise, enthralled by her competence as she slipped a small but swift outboard motor – *from where?*- into its appointed slot.

EEEEEEEEEEEEEEEEEEEEEEEEEEEEEEEEEE as we whipped over the waves, cold sea spray coating her blouse, hardening her nipples atop the globe puppies ... we roared over the early border of the sandbar shore, as the craft beached.

She kissed me as she strode by, heaving an onboard package to the beach. Standing above it she pressed a knob and the package began to self-inflate just as the Zodiac had ... until a full size tent stood there resplendent in the light, rising breeze.

I was spellbound with admiration, archetype warrior woman! Leyna fancied herself an emerging photographer, extracting an impressive Nikon from her elaborate pack, she snapped me in various poses, with sunglasses and an illegal switchblade, peeking over the sand like a cocktail of Clockwork Orange and Kilroy.

I worshiped her. The light began to meter down, fading into a lovely distant fire glow. We retreated into the mechanized tent, laid down and began to mate.

Then in the moment of ecstasies' tonguing ... EPHIPANY ... a blinding summation of meteoric cranial firecracker

213

stimuli and evidence: scars, errant vaginal plumbing, the strong facial cast and fantastic South American ripe breasts that made my nursing lips purse… holy mother of Christ!

I was on a tiny granular island, captive to a transsexual immediately post op! You must remember even breast augmentation was nouveau then, although rampant in the southern continent. The piranha scars were skin grafts! I was seized, wild eyed, near cryogenic for a moment … my saliva suddenly bitter, metallic with revulsion. I smiled with childish endearment; an actor *elevates with the spontaneous fizz.*

How could I get off that fucking sandbar!!!?

I grasped my chest and fell backward feigning an epileptic seizure! I manifested foam at my lips, alternatingly writhing, bucking and shivering my hips.

"Hospital!!!" I shrieked, low raspy whimpering.

With combat medic like precision she/he wrapped me in a blanket, deflated the elaborate tent structure and manfully loaded all as I propelled my fit to continuing and ascending urgency, eyes bugged, gagging demi suffocation. She wrapped me in her embrace and placed me tenderly in the bow … pushed us off …

EEEEEEEEEEEEEEEEEEEEEEEEEEEEEEEEEEEEEEE EEEEEE catching airborne from waves in now rainbow wedding of sea and sky, mist moisture on my brow only adding to the illusion of fevered incapacity. Her/his steely solicitation and determination to save her paramour!

We soar to the landing; in gastrointestinal turmoil I wretch, drool, stumble from the craft as she pushes the button necessary to reduce the Zodiac to its suitcase configuration, her deft slam packing replaces the machine in its storage womb within the supercar trunk.

Wheels churn, gravel splatters in a wide comet, the 12-cylinder 469 horses burble howl as we flash fan out on ungodly expensive hi-pro radials from the parking lot and enter LIE at first responder speed.

I spit a bit on the dash and luminous dials, clearly losing the struggle, last ditch grip to life.

The New York hospital looms, Oz-like on the horizon, my Bolivian hybrid wrenches the wheel authoritatively - no doubt a tier one graduate of Bob Bondurant Racing School - squeal weaves the car to the emergency room double doors.

I roll from the barely stopped car, collide with doors in a headlong plunge to medical attention. She moves away quickly to park the vehicle.

I fled through the hospital corridors, cascading through doors and exited into an alley. I move off into urban steel and walls, an ape joining the upright.

*****

I was playing with fabulous images – matching copy to LIFE Magazine's history of war coverage that would emerge later within SAVING PRIVATE RYAN ... to

INTERVIEW, the most influential purveyor of photographic societal shifts with Warhol, driven by Perry Ellis, Ralph Lauren, Calvin Klein and the brilliant editorial eye of Robert Hayes.

Robert would be dead by 1980, a first casualty of the ravages to the secret plague. He shielded his writers (including the fitfully alcoholic pill popping Truman Capote) from morons and their snorting sycophantic subterranean jealousies.

"We should do a story about you!" was Andy's usual glazed quip to everyone in virtually any situation. He viewed all human encounters as "cruising". Uniquely vacuous inanities of Andy.

Celebrity interviews were swift and profitable. In acknowledgement to my lofty TIME, INC. residency Hayes paid me four times the going rate ($200 per rather than the usual $50) as he set me onto Che Guevara's sister Celia, when I saw she was in Chicago to bring international attention to the 20,000 Argentinian 'Los Desaparecidos' - murdered nuns, priests, unionists, teachers, butchered at the hands of the military junta … Rebecca Wright, waif principal American Ballet Theater dancer with whom I had a brief affair … Rutger Hauer at the dawn of his leading man stardom for the movie SOLDIER OF ORANGE … quintessential Californian Bruce Penhall, world Motocross champion, fashion prince Ellis and Ted Turner at the onset of CNN – also now a fallen network by its left leaning.

*Were it not for the rise of FOX NEWS, how much more
'progressive' might the national conversation have
descended – CNN remains nearly simply a daily reading in
DNC propaganda.*

I was appropriately under the influence of Oriana Fallaci,
fearless Italian anti-fascist and anti-Islamist journalist, a
woman who bared her strong voice and eye on many of the
megalomaniacal political people of the time.

Turner threatened to terminate his interview when I
challenged his lady killer reputation on the basis of
fairness.

"What would you do if your wife had a reputation as a
man hunter?"

The absurdity and naiveté I exhibited - actually possessing
the notion INTERVIEW could represent a place for real
'journalism' rather than the abject celebrity PR it truly
embodied in the age of Baba Walters.

It was a weird time as I did my research (not nearly as
weird as in Argentina) – backing up facts of the kidnapped
and butchered - the CIA believing I was a revolutionary,
the Left convinced I was a CIA informant.

That was the first time Colacello fired me for 'communist
propaganda' – *actually scrawled across the top of the piece
in red pen.* I had scooped the media world by two years. He
was petrified of offending Rockefellers who were building
a nuclear power plant for the junta daisy chain of dictators.

Colacello blithely sold the corpses of 20,000 slaughtered into oblivion for the sake of social cachet, truly a special media ugly duckling in a fecal laden pond. He was forced to rehire me publicly when three days later my Ted Turner interview was so well received – never forgave me for that sin.

What people never realized was Warhol's primary and primal fear: he was poised and running from the next Holocaust. That's why shadow Andy cultivated the sons and daughters of old Wasp money – he felt these alliances/dalliances might shelter him as a Jew.

Gentleman bi-sexual friend and fellow Virginian Perry Ellis died swiftly of AIDS as Hayes had, his personal fortune mushrooming, just as he was breaking free from bankers and backers he was gone. I owed him $1700 at the time; to repay the debt posthumously I volunteered for a bit at an AIDS charity in Los Angeles.

I lost my best friend Marcus similarly a bit later. He was a lot of people's best friend. I never even knew Marcus was bi-sexual – he had let caution fly to the wind in sexual liberation over a summer or two. Marcus, an actor angel who never made it from the catering earn-extra scene that spawned Lawrence Bender - Quentin Tarantino's producer – and myself when I parachuted from stratospheric advertising/journalism to theatrical study.

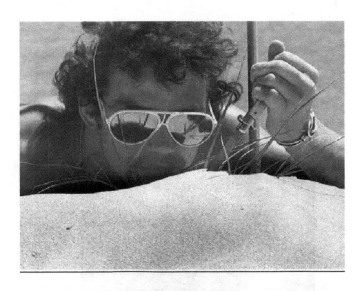

Moments from feigning epilepsy to escape amorous Bolivian tranny on Long Island sand barge...

Will BLUEBOY pay me $10,000 if I pull off my rugger jersey?

Shaft drive, elegance and torque – I can make you come at 175mph.

BLUEBOY unclothed

BLUEBOY clothed

Twenty: Correspondent

"I'm sorry! I couldn't find a pulse. You were so cold!"
Dr. Phillip Carroll / TALES FROM THE DARKSIDE

Up the tiers of advertising I went, never holding a job
beyond eight months or so, my salary accelerating higher
by transitory considered movement, leap frogging from
agency to magazine as if they were lily pads.

At the same time, I was a 'checkered' man – on the one
hand, integrity driven, craft obsessed, an expansive work
ethic, on the other hand morally flawed infidel/low level
con.

Chief among my sins: ruthless cad to an innocent admiral's
daughter (another of the dropped adoring Richmond young
women after a semester of sexual awakening), and once in
New York pulling American Express/Bank of America
Travelers' check scams.

While on the shoot for the BLUEBOY/PLAYGIRL
centerfold I lifted a $200,000 Albert Vargas painting from
PLAYBOY.

Being service/lust oriented – I had some redemptive future
acting 'exposure' when I became the designated lover for
an American sweetheart Academy Award winning wife of
a beloved Parkinson's riddled stage/screen/television
writer. John Tillinger an actor becoming a Broadway
director force - three hit shows at once and one in the West
End of London – set this interlude up.

On more than one occasion others would advertise my dick deftness to some woman in crisis and off I'd go dashing to the gap once more. It wasn't callous, actually deeply, warmly human – creatures finding their way, attempting to fulfill long loyalties while whispering breath to embers of desperate, critical desires.

I simultaneously conceived journalistic device for reporting assignments. (I would ask questions of and give answers from zenith inanimate objects – 'interview' Maud Frizon shoes, chat with a Ducati 900 175mph motorcycle, converse with proto-organic Chateau Vignelaure French wine.)

I was hired to create ad promotion campaigns by an executive moving to PLAYBOY. I didn't really care for the job, all figures and killer products, cigarettes and the more likeable liquor. No bunnies, simply a breed of old school ad sales hacks in need of stratospheric demographic bullshit to pull in the pages.

One of PLAYBOY'S more intriguing ads was for something called an 'Auto Suck', an instrument one plugged into the cigarette lighter while in traffic, then placed the receptacle end on one's penis and I suppose one was quickly, mechanically brought to culmination.

The weird part was it had dual receptacles, ready-made for dude couples intent on driving while impaired by spasmodic sensation. Odd ad placement in the palace of hetero fantasy. Another exemplary ad touted a full body rubber suit. "Feel the Sensual Feel of 100% Rubber!"

The Columbia University rugby team was taking a tour of the Caribbean. They needed extra players to round out the squad. The enchantment of southern climes for a New England and Virginia bred pupa was irresistible.

I had no fascination for traditional European excursions, wishing to be a cowboy rather than a sophisticate. Thompson had gone south, Hemmingway went to Cuba. I sauntered into the senior PLAYBOY hack, a good spirit, asked for time off for the rugby tour. He said, "Sure and keep going. Fuck you, you're fired!" I went in and packed up the Albert Vargas original in my office (stunning illustrative art was omnipresent throughout PLAYBOY) and left the building.

Wandering Manhattan open-mouthed, idiotic for several hours, I made my way to several magazines, told them I was going to South America. Did they want articles on cocaine and sports?

I knew some hang glider pilots who were going to compete in the World Championships in Argentina, pitched senior editors on 'free sport in thug regime', threw violent coke trade in for added panache.

Truth be told I had a wild instinct to sample pure coke at the source. The magazines gave me 'kill fees', $500 nonrefundable advance against $3,000-$5,000 per piece. I was, after all, a young knight who had conjured hi-level advertising for nearly every Big Apple mag. Not everyone was allowed to launch LIFE!

Two days later I was in Bogota, Colombia, a city, in 1978, of starving dogs wandering ruins sniffing sewage for flesh.

Every bar, restaurant, courtyard, mall, every open space, had a blood-stained chalk outline of a body. They settled *everything* mano a mano with knives or AK-47's – standard equipment in vehicles of all males, local teenagers to the elderly.

The Army – slack-jawed Mestizo Indian youth from the mountain poor, distinct from the urban dwellers with their Castilian Spanish features sipping café con leche – were on each corner with automatic weapons.

I hooked up with a cadre of moneyed Venezuelans whose families owned 80% of the region's cheese trade.

They had cash and testosterone, hang gliding and paragliding into ramshackle villages where campesinos viewed them as released god souls falling from the heavens.

Incarnate, ascending.

An Ice Skating acrobat troupe of firm bodied gays and young women was running a parallel tour on the ground, performing in bull rings transformed by flooding the bowls with gritty aqua, *then freezing*. The issue of sand tripping up the skaters was ongoing.

I began an affair with the brunette mother hen of the skaters - *inserting tango vanilla into Queen of Ice Show Babes* - applying salve to her abrasions post extravaganza and pre-coital.

The two groups made their zig-zag way about the once rich (now bankrupt and leveled 'socialist experiment') Venezuelan countryside absorbing the adoration of the rural aboriginals.

Once I crossed over to Colombia security was a primary concern for the populace. Crime was rampant.

Everyman's Catholic castle a walled compound, barb wired, alarmed and armed.

The Colombian law at the time allowed recreational possession of up to two ounces of coke. Cannabis, a throw away in coke transactions, zip-locked football size golden bagged trifles to cement deals, dangerous to smoke in the hotels because of pungent odor and the presence of a multitude of undercover informants preying on foreigners and their Colombian avatars.

Coke in this milieu became no more expensive - $9 a gram for purest - than today's daily coffee. I did it as morning, noon and night energy enhancement. Naturally as my dependence grew, paranoia blossomed as well.

I picked up a pack of Christmas cards and carefully placed a gram or two in 17 different Santa Claus /Christ manger messages, all addressed to various New York City and Connecticut friends. Each arrived unmolested, enough cocaine back home to alter the minor barter economies gyrating around me – rent, groceries, cocktails and dining, experiential parties, furious pushup contests high on whippet cannisters and making love with a Queens voluptuary named Jessica.

*****

Hearing illicit, imaginary sounds come from the walls,
furiously typing, tooting away in ersatz Kerouac manner, I
decided one night to take a break from my confining room
at the Hotel Continental in downtown Bogota.

Slamming up a bon voyage line the size of a boa
constrictor, I made my way down the hall, descending in
the elevator, out into the lobby filled with short men in dark
suits, white shirts, black tie, socks and shoes, each adorned
by a Pancho Villa moustache.

All these slick, squinting dilated eyes turned toward me as I
exited the elevator.

I stood still, assembling my breath, back into the elevator,
punched my floor button and rose up slowly, hum of the
machine abnormally loud. At my floor I moved silently off.
Nearing the turn in the hall to my room, I peered around the
corner and saw two short suits in the initial stage of jacking
open the door to my room.

I backed up slightly, coughed loudly, came around the
corner as they moved away from my door quickly and
began striding down the hall away from me.

I opened my room door, hurried, gathered the two ounces
of pure powder, and shoved it into a pocket of the ski vest I
was wearing, locked the door, moved quickly down the
hall, into throbbing elevator, down to the garish lobby,
sliding through, past the mob of staring stubby, clearly
policeman/functionary hombres.

I fast walked to the entrance, out into the night, dove into a taxi with the omnipresent elaborate mural of Che, 'Conquest of the People!' scrawled in Colombian along its '50's body, 30-foot antenna lashed front to rear.

We accelerated away, turning in the rear window I caught the cadre of Napoleon high suited men scurry from hotel, colliding into one another, scrambling too numerously into another taxi with bright, garish depictions of bolo slinging vaqueros galloping the pampas.

They powered up behind us.

This went on all over the city, we'd hit traffic, the suited ones would disgorge from their vehicle, rush my car, my cab driver – increasingly petrified at what the hell he had gotten himself into - would gas lunge for an opening, barely scoot away, suits ridiculously running back to their car, another interval of pursuit.

I'd had enough.

I flipped Bolivars at the driver, rolled from the cab, took off at a rugby run between cars spray painted with Bolivar and the Madonna. ... vectored into an alley at full speed, *into a 20-foot wall.* I went over it like it was four feet, onto the burnt umber tiled roof of a building, bolting forward, the tile roof exploded downward as if set with charges, collapsing me into an elegant restaurant, a well-appointed dining room of moneyed patrons, sipping wine, nibbling squab, seducing each other.

There were screams as I erupted downward into the room, flailing my appendages in all directions for a grip, tile shrapnel flying violently.

The large Bowie style diving knife I kept strapped to my calf flipped loose, skittering across the floor. I lunged for it and came up startled, snarling, razor edged blade extended. The patrons reacted of course with mortal terror, certain I was there to butcher them. Couples and families wailed and wept at higher pitch, crashing away, chairs flung about, wine glasses dishes fragmenting, panic in their eyes.

Out the door, I moved swiftly to the city university center. Lost among the students I stashed the two ounces in an open janitor's closet.

Returning quietly to the Hotel Continental, I slept the night. At dawn I slipped back over to the university, retrieved the coke quickly, broke for the sea coast and the oldest city of the western hemisphere.

Cartagena, ancient fortress city atop all of South America, the Ft. Knox of Spanish Conquistadors stockpiling looted Inca gold.

The plunder was loaded by slaves aboard lumbering, heavily armed galleon convoys to make its way to Spain through pirate riddled waters.

It is a city of sensory salve and restoration, a world apart from the urban blight of Bogota.

The top of the wide high walls of the citadel, once braced with bronze and steel state of the art 16th century artillery,

were transformed in the modern era into a two lane
highway circumventing the ciudad.

Each day Colombian anteaters, miraculously slow, make
their slothful way to the chlorinated hotel pools throughout
the palmed, pristine beached city.

Waiters, bartenders and hoteliers, shop keepers, prostitutes
and artists keep vigil, wait and watch until the snouted
beasts arrive to drink at each turquoise adulterated body of
captive liquid.

Just as the anteaters nearly achieve their dream sip, which
would spell their death from the treated water, the polyglot
of beast benefactors swoop in and pluck/carry the thirsty
creatures to the far borders of their individual grounds.

As one, the anteaters wheel, turn and begin the pilgrimage
once more ... love of deathly water. Kind of like addicts
relentlessly returning to the killing slough of sex, drugs and
action.

In those days my member flicked out as often as the sloth's
tongue. There was no thought or discussion of girlfriend or
boyfriend, marriage or eternal pairing.

The notion of fidelity was non-existent, a game of
lovemaking, conquest of gender, loot of pussy, tits and
mouths, tresses and limbs.

Always saved from final poison of banality, ever plying
froth covered liquids for sex gems and memory.

Three years later in self inspired passage to absolution –
after carrying that unwieldy Vargas painting around with
me everywhere, Barabbas carrying his cross, I pulled a
night break into the PLAYBOY building and returned the
painting. When I went outside the air was clean and bright
in the Big Apple. I wept, and God is my witness Whitney
Houston's "The Greatest Love of All" was playing on the
street.

I traveled long distance by train to return piece by piece the
shoplifted gear.

Never been a thief since – except I steal politically
corrupt/biased mags like ROLLINGSTONE, NEW YORK,
VANITY FAIR AND NEW YORKER et al from doctors'
offices. It's my small way of sifting and keeping pace with
the 50% propaganda, 30% PR puff, 10%
enlightenment/journalism/entertainment - know thy enemy
without bolstering their bottom line.

Twenty-One: Joys and Treacheries

"I'm Just a Regular Joe, Providing a Public Service."
Randall Cooper / X-FILES

Initially I had been less than serious about a gorgeous Israeli I met, despite her crafted body and lean feminine scale, full breasts and raven hair, dark Sephardic eyes watching me throughout Manhattan. The reason for my reticence was she was married. I had momentarily had enough of 'poking' into the matrimonial matches of others.

A recent tryst with a rugby player's *wife and mistress* had raked my affinity for emotional attachment to wives.

Arriving back from South America, where in retrospect I was lucky to survive, I flew to Los Angeles to close out a piece on a hang glider test pilot who plummeted from the top of Angel Falls in Venezuela.

Rick Piccirilli, interesting cat, invented a parachute that would open below 600 feet, a necessity if one was to escape death in a collapsing hang glider. It's important to note that this was prior to the days of soft airfoil paragliders, mid-air structural failures were common.

I was given the name of a fellow rugger in Santa Monica. In rugby all are brothers and reciprocal hospitality is the expected norm. Normally that doesn't extend to dick downing the wife.

The rugger graciously picked me up from LA International. I was whisked to his home to meet wife and sweet young kids.

The party in my honor was initiated. Among the revelers was a slightly older dark MILF.

No, not the Israeli vixen. This is before the Israeli, another deep dish.

The wife of the rugger brother was a doll as well and despite a momentary pang of regret for her married status, I appropriately *(opportunistically)* swiveled my attention to the brunette friend.

As it happened, she and I were sharing separate couches in the living room. Post festivities, all parties said, 'sweet dreams,' wife and the rugger waving before they disappeared into the master bedroom. The MILF and I waved across the 10 feet separating the couches, lights were turned off and I mused in the dark.

Honor, of course, dictated no further thought of the fetching wife, so why not gambol with my sultry 'couch mate?' It was a short jaunt for the parched anteater to sip and splash within her pink waterhole. Never one to forego pleasure I made the portage to the land of delicious.

By day, I chatted with Piccirilli and fleshed out the article. At night, I found myself watching TV with wife and low and behold she began dragging me to her bracing inland sea.

I was shocked but rolled with it. I felt the onrush of chlorinated love since it was the wife to whom I was first powerfully attracted.

All of this came to a head when the rugger came bursting in just as the wife was mounting me.

"Don't let me interrupt! Keep your hard on there!" He screamed as he violently opened and slammed shut drawers looking for god knows what.

While I was fumbling and contrite, wife became enraged and verbally assaulted the rugger hubby, cursing him. I was enthralled and astounded at her bravado. The rugger wilted at her rage and left as rapidly as he had arrived.

How could I not be spun rapt by this firebrand lass? She was the living adage 'the best defense is a spirited offense'.

As she resumed making love to me, the whole 'payback' scheme was revealed, poetry slam from her lips as she pulverized the raw sugar mill.

The rugger hubby had been caught in an affair with the wife's best friend, the comely couch rider who I had recently fucked, so the wife had an agreed upon 'payback chip' and I was it.

Not one to be unaware of ribald Alpha male irony or to pass up poaching in ponds, I primitively savored the jeweled reality of having fucked the man's mistress and wife in less than 24 hours ... a true sloth wallowing not just in some shallow estuary but diving deep through dual waterfalls.

None of this has any lasting value other than titillation and brutal reinforcement of the truism that if you don't want your woman conjoining the beast of two backs with another man then don't toss the spice rack to another woman. But of course, this whetting of affections and embraces is what makes the world go round.

After three days of non-stop in her charms, I departed Los Angeles feeling 'used'.

I know it's idiotic! What did I expect, the woman to leave her family, to dash her kids against the reef of our interlude?

In any case that's why I ludicrously vowed never to become involved with a married woman ever again. A vow, like most my vows (save delivering the goods as man and artist), I was sweetly destined not to keep.

I would soon fling myself into the arms of the Israeli as I would many wives tip toeing on the precipice of the divorce abyss.

Twenty-Two: Adore Tripping

"Stay put Boy Scout. Come with me Princess." Lyle Gutherie / WALKER, TEXAS RANGER

There were several years we did everything under hallucinogenic power.

Mescaline, mushrooms, psilocybin and Acid - I recommend doing so (if at all) with Ken Keseyian exhilaration and Paul Horning, Jim Brown steam roller athleticism, the take one to give one bravado of UFC's Matt Brown and Thiago Silva (expelled for stimulant fueled criminality), Robbie Lawler's aggressive willingness to trade punishment, T.J. Dillishaw's and Carlos Condit's aerial multidimensional nimbleness and intelligent courage, Rory McDonald's screw driver technical proficiency.

If you don't know what this paragraph means, can't decipher it, let it be said simply that one should not do hallucinogens without intelligence, abandon, attitude and markedly healthy constitution.

Motorcycling on acid, depth of field ... a wild, exaggerated focus, acid hallucinations dropping away and one is left with a methamphetamine feel, useful, protective ... smoothly to the bike's rhythms and perfectly remembered, swift circling of the internal shaft, quickness as cinema passing freshens the spirit and goes into a forward cranial room, blip, blip, snap canvas or is that time itself? The caressing slap and slash of leather to leather ... slowing, color and humbling beauty, distance betrayed ... easing to a stop a 1/2 mile from a glowing red light, alert, alive, daft mastery.

Skiing and tripping … turning is a revelation after one or two lessons, this terror filled, luxuriously-spellbinding downhill freshness is at last somehow other than a suicide plummet, an aerodynamic gripping balance to the bottom, then a wrenching shift, snow plume fanning wide, bringing yourself in for the crash or a glory slide.

On the other hand, baseball cannot be recommended while tripping, New England colors bursting and beautiful catching bullet hit fast balls at any position enthralled by mescaline, LSD, peyote, psilocybin, DMT, PCP is laughably challenging … take yourself out of the game, ignore the perplexed gawking of teammates.

When I think of that hallucinogenic time … the Israeli who fused with me, she and I tripping near this Maine wooded lake all day, parts of the Moto Guzzi engine tapping nearby, forest glimmering and pure. Late in the afternoon, from the black water, two men in ancient deep-sea salvage rigs randomly emerged, risen from fresh water depths.

What? Alone in the woods and here comes Captain Nemo's minions.

I had met the Israeli at a restaurant ahead of its time with organic cocktails. She was a diplomat's wife getting by as a waitress. My nostrils flared - body bonfire exchange between us.

All of us know when we collide with our lovers, we sense the coming upheaval, wrenching of lives and pheromone swooning. When she left her husband, rendering her an illegal alien, she got her own place.

She was learning English from slogans on TV – "You Got It Toyota!" I moved in out of sheer expediency when I popped back from Los Angeles. All my male friends' wandering girlfriends seemed to want to cohabitate suddenly. I was the third wheel across town. I needed a place, nothing more.

Within 48 hours I was headlong in love, giving her orgasms by seizing her ankles in my mouth, and every other way possible. Love wildfire arson.

Months later -

"Can I become a call girl?" She asked this, to my naïve sensibility, romantically. I empathized with her frustration while waitressing, her inability to work except in cash clubs. She wanted to contribute despite my easy abilities covering us with my writing.

For me nothing could separate us, divide the physical and emotional eternal bonds … how idiotic of me.

We lived then in a lovely fishermen's cottage on Long Island Sound with a pet rabbit named Velvetino. I had no idea I was horribly allergic to the bunny. Wracking asthmatic struggles happened daily in between our passing out making love.

She's gone now, a memory hallucination ... a onetime stunning merger of physical lust and emotional love, causing both of us to lose consciousness entangled in each other's bodies ... before materialism and the money necessary to straighten out her immigration became vital. She came in late at night and took me in her mouth while I awoke slowly, and she whispered, "We are the only pure thing," as she sucked.

One day she gave me $500 dollars in a tiny Japanese restaurant ... proceeds from her first and only John, a billionaire ... to celebrate we made love standing up in the micro bathroom.

Israeli and I would torque away north or east on the Moto Guzzi, the north to New England routes winding and sweeping, or the Long Island Expressway bee line to the beach, the front spear wheel of the bike tenuous with the road as the speed climbed to the sky.

We came to a possum, hit and run, back broken and crippled. I couldn't unpack the survival .22 rifle. It's illegal to shoot on or from a road except in the rural West - *the coolest and most readily productive elk hunts happen dismounted from an old pickup immediately after a snow storm in Montana.* Go to the nearest farmhouse, ask permission to hunt and the landowners always say yes!

But we were east of New York City now, and not wishing the possum to suffer, I picked up the creature by the tail and mortally smashed his skull on the asphalt with a long Hi Lai arc of my arm.

The killing's decisiveness made the Israeli wet with desire and turmoil for years. The best women seem to like those capable of calculated killing. I get it, here's a man that can go forth and pull down the woolly mammoth for its flesh without help from the village.

Later, when we were shooting coke intravenously and after a spectacular crash on the Moto Guzzi, our arousal derailed, our connection forever split. She terminated us as swiftly and brutally as I had the possum, gone, fled to the billionaire… a lesson in the tenuous nature of eternal love, the character splintering potential of drug decadence and the certain, loving ride of time sending us on our way to higher purpose.

From heartache comes a bright strobing future.

Twenty-Three: Let Them Know You by Your Work

"My dear Pip, a kiss isn't going to do it. She's an orphan with an orphan's disease. She's not going to be fixed." – Byron Volpe / PARASOMNIA

A gay, Nazi astrologer, interior designer con man – Freddy, long ago financially disgraced and dead of AIDS - once told me, as he introduced me to New York elite society, "Let them know you by your work."

As he ushered me around Studio 54, past the decorative translucent, horse tethered in the lobby, he pointed out, "She's the wife of the Prime Minister and she's letting truck drivers up her mini skirt. He's a Senator from New York and he's into boys of indeterminate legality. I'm telling you this so you never feel insecure around these people. They are flawed as we all are. And you? You're the Hemingway of your era. You're a writer from TIME!"

He was given to hyperbole but all of them were mad for publicity and fame. TIME offered that promise, I was treated with acceptance and deference.

*****

I saw all the great fights of the Ali era … iconic warriors: Frazier, Forman, Ken Norton, Wepner. One night, Nassau Coliseum, George Foreman nearly killed Joe Frasier – hung him up on the corner stanchions and busted him up even after he was unconscious, lifted his entire body off the floor with primordial uppercuts.

I met Ali three times. He published a book; as a writer, I was invited to a small Manhattan party given by his publishing house.

I can't tell you what that meant to me, the prospect of seeing him, speaking with the Lord of ring and rebellion. I had adored him from the time he took out Sonny Liston when I was thirteen. I knew he would win even as the world considered him sacrificial carrion. He was the cool verbal iconoclast of the age, hero to a young man away from home and failing in school.

I went to the party, a small room. The only large people – publishing is not known for big dudes – were Ali, Joe Frazier, a New York Giant football player and myself grown into full physical power. I got in the short line with the literary folks to get The Greatest's autograph, to mumble something in his presence.

It became my turn. I stepped forward to my hero. He turned his face away with an expression of disdain and refused to speak to me. I stood there awkwardly confused. Why? I walked away, no autograph, no memorable words, embarrassed, quivering strangely and rippling with hurt.

My creative director, mentor Roy Beauchamp, offered this. "Who knows what a large white man means to him." Who is the racist? Where is the racism in America? I could still do nothing but love him.

*****

Went to Yankee Stadium the night that Ali and Ken Norton
fought for the heavyweight crown. The House that Ruth
built was overflowing volcanically with people, fans falling
off top tiers, a hundred thousand beings screaming for two
gladiators.

ALLLLLLLLLLLIIIIIIII!!!!!!!!!!!!!! Latinos, a cry like
primal war wails of an entire people, Ali Ali Ali Ali Ali Ali
Ali Ali Ali Ali Ali Ali!!!!! Blacks! Caribe, White and
Arab, Puerto Rico to Moscow.

Concentric rings coming from the small square at the center
were seething with people, agitated, enflamed. Nearest to
the ring, on the actual infield of the baseball diamond,
$1,000 seats were possessed by men in peak suits, their
bombshell peaches of the 20th century, furs and diamonds,
peek-a-boo bodies in fabric.

Movie comets, politicians, press, the finest athletes from
sport, shakers from mobsters and moneyed tycoons, molls
and models.

Ali was escorted everywhere, guarded 24 hours a day,
Nation of Islam's large specimens of erect black masculine
perfection, and minions of murderous Elijah Mohammed.
Each was in a perfectly tailored brown suit, white shirt and
dark tie. Free from drugs, prison and poverty, fanatical in
the black movement and American Allah's embrace.

Thousands were cocooning the ring, fifty yards deep.

Outward into mid-range seats - upper middle class of New York – a swelling, seething ring of beer and whiskey stockbrokers, lawyers, flight attendant dates, cocktailed up semi-civilized expression of society able to afford two hundred-dollar seats – over the floor of the entire teeming field.

Stadium seats began to climb, skyward and away, socio economic order descended, class elevator downward. Ticket price descending; education down, higher and higher into cheap seats.

Working class tickets, retail, sanitation, subway workers, shop girls, off duty cops and taxi drivers, hotel workers, bar men & maids.

Twenty-five dollars scraped from boring jobs, grandma's medicine money, supplemented by minor drug deals, all to view two daemons below.

Scrambling, riotously happy simply to be there, to high five each other and clap each other on the back, suck down Colt .45 and scarf shit hot dogs, swilling wine from screw top bottles and dragging on skunk Mexican pot, jostling each other in rare perfectly crystalline New York air.

People clinging to the rim. Over the edge of the stadium the lights of the city gleamed like eternal ornaments. Jets soared from La Guardia, Kennedy and Newark, trailed above and across the ink of the sky to the world beyond.

It was like nothing so much as being at the vortex of a South American revolution.

ALLLLLLLLLLLLLLIIIIIIIIIIIIIIIIIIIIIII!!!!!!!!!!!
KENNNNIIIIIIIIIIIIIIIIIIIII!!!!! NORTON! NORTON!
NORTON!!!!!

Norton always possessed the most chiseled sculptured body of the sport. He was the true black Adonis of the age, power of an NFL fullback with Mr. Olympia scale in every smooth, striated muscle of his body. And this night was his most luminous moment in the time of his manhood.

Ali and Norton clashed for fifteen rounds of brutal exchange. I will always believe that Norton won, but the unwritten rule that one must decisively beat a champion to take his belt prevailed.

And of course, too, it was Ali, the Prince. One couldn't almost beat Ali, one must leave no doubt.

I embrace the theory that Ali ultimately lost the most there. Certainly, the later Frazier bouts drove him toward tremors and Parkinson's, but I believe damage to his wiring system began that turbulent night in Yankee Stadium.

They fought, Ali in his white trunks, Norton in black. They summoned all that a man has to call upon (save war) through numbing fatigue, pain and courage.

When it was over, the epic decision rung, Nation of Islam cadres raised Ali above them Christ-like, his arms falling limp beneath him.

They carried him from the ring, crowd in mass hysteria of adoration. Each Muslim, to a man, pulled out a wooden truncheon and, as a mob, they beat their way through to create passage for their Messiah, their validating Emperor, through diamond clad honeys and fat cats, wailed with their clubs at heads, smashed chairs as society's crème fled before them.

From the ring they came slashing. The phalanx turned and crushed its way the entire circle of the stadium floor - a savage victory lap stomping all in its path as the stadium of 100,000 cells is becoming one body, one organism of reverence and ecstasy, one eruption in exaltation to the idol Ali. Christ was going home. This man was going home. Mohammed Ali was simply going home from work.

Let them know you by your work.

I met Ali a second time on a street corner near 42nd street after his career in the ring had ascended, then descended, perhaps too long, beyond endurance and passage of years and body.

I rounded the granite building and there he was - against the building, simply standing as the masses teemed by him.

"What are you doing here?" I asked. "Just standing here?"

"I like the people," he said quietly. He smiled at me and thumped me on the shoulder. "I like to feel the people."

*****

The third time, most recently, though they are both gone now, I hit a small party in southern California and there he was. The Parkinson's symptoms were advanced. He sat quietly, and we warmly spoke. He was gentle, gracious and at peace, or so it seemed.

Nearby Ken Norton sat. I moved to him, chatted with him as well. We made plans for an interview. A year or so before Norton's car had gone airborne on an LA freeway at 90mph, careening into a concrete wall. Ken had shattered nearly every bone in his ebony body. He was still large, now his gait was the movement of a man broken, reassembled, still moving forward. His son was in the NFL.

Two titans in a room, each humbled by life and time.

One quintessential story and film of Ali and Norton has not yet been told.

We know of Ali's triumphs – Michael Mann's ALI and the great documentary WHEN WE WERE KINGS - but what of the story of the greatest athlete in human history, the most famous man of all, who must descend to frailty, immobility and then death as we must all.

What of the Norton mythos of the champion with the most symmetrically perfect body in sports who must climb a mountain each moment simply to walk again?

Alright, let them know you by your work.

Years later I briefly dated Veronica Porsche, Ali's former wife, eternal beauty that collided with his marriage in Zaire. She was at last transforming herself from Muslim subservient wife to psychologist.

She came to my place as I was writing one day and spoke elegantly of her need to remain free as this long-deferred metamorphosis continued. I understood, she had stood so long in the shadows of men that she could not risk another submersion into love.

I am not a man who asks a woman to stand in the shadows, I revel in the full ascension of people regardless of race, creed, gender, sexual persuasion, religion – the American ideal beyond Jeffersonian life and into 21st century reality. Simultaneously I abhor identity politics, exclusion and compartmentalization of the American dream.

Women's empowerment? Yes! But what of maligned fathers, diminished boys?

Race? Let all who perpetrate institutional racism know they face a formidable foe in their midst – me. But also let all those who do not look to themselves and acknowledge self-accountability in a free and available world – professional victims will not be countenanced.

And it is not healthy to bestow that upon children, the conceit that one is either disadvantaged or victimized from birth.

Those made 'uncomfortable' by speech will be scoffed at, those who do not participate in debate are to be maligned and called trivial.

It's about PEOPLE and justice folks – decent, fair and rational on the one side ... corrupt, stifling and lying on the other.

Projection is afoot in America. The diseased heaping their own pathology against those who disagree.

Do I need to listen and evolve? You bet. We all must together in action and thought.

Twenty-Four: Bored at the Pinnacle

"I stop at the first red light. The guy behind me yells 'If you're gonna stop at every red light we're never gonna get anywhere'." Al Humphries / SOLDIER OF FORTUNE, INC.

I was lolling at one cathedral of the New York advertising game.

A highly paid writer at TIME INC., with extraordinary benefits and an expense account for any restaurant in New York.

I possessed near civil service stability, tenure and seniority, couldn't be fired except for some highly public deviancy, a promotion - lateral or otherwise - more likely.

I was bored – surrounded by well meaning, lovable, upper strata educational elite.

"The only thing a Yale or Harvard degree gave one was the ability to flee through the halls with your preppie tie flapping."

I looked around, at best I could see my becoming one of many Vice Presidents. The older guys I saw seemed diminished, fearfully pathetic.

My boss man mentor called me into his office and said I might have his job as Creative Director within the year if I merely made the decision to remain. The air was still for a moment. I looked out the wide window view of the city scape in wide screen panorama and said, "I guess I'll go."

He was appalled, a bit hurt, protégé leaving Yoda but so it goes. The greatest sin for protégé was boredom, creative and otherwise.

Our little galaxy of TIME INC. was shocked. It was inexplicable madness to leave to all save one elderly secretary, executive assistant to head pooh bah. She asked me, "Why are you leaving?" and I replied, "I just don't belong here." She smiled wistfully, pleased. "Good," she said firmly, as if knowing the inherent failure, the impotent decay in staying there, and the gift of launching into unknown.

I left cold two weeks later, not knowing what was next.

Twenty-Five: Zone of Bells/Room of See Saws

"He's dialed in … we have all points of entrance under surveillance, from roof top to sewer system." Haggerty/ ERASER

What was truly next was rash cocaine consumption by injection during a 4-month period previously alluded to.

I took a professional zig-zag as co-creative director of a small boutique agency handling icons like Maud Frizon and Givenchy.

My partner, Hasidic, diabetic, vegetarian, a highly-delicate coke fiend with an endless supply of fresh medicinal needles and fully attuned visual arts sensibility.

He's dead now. His frail, European designer-clad body destroyed by the onslaught of boosted pure white Bolivian snow.

Models and blow, pre-set diabetic needles in every pocket, on my way to couture shoots in Martinique, or lower Manhattan, mile high sex during flights to locations in Jamaica.

Those of you who know, know. Injected cocaine is infinite joy and endless hell twenty minutes later as the precipitous descent radically and instantly asserts itself. Not mid paragraph, not mid-sentence, but mid letter, mid lip utterance … a person goes from best, most simpatico soul amigo or lover to the most inconsequential piece of dung standing in the way of "MORE! MORE! MORE!"

Ever the purist I would mix Italian San Pellegrino Flat Water, a touch of organic honey and bring it to a boil in a pristine spoon. A bunny tail of purist organic cotton for straining purposes, a pinch of tested, vetted coke, the brilliant needle beak dipping in the milky fluid, the popping elimination of the bubbles from the skyward needle lance. Poised over the vein, tied off with a fleur-de-lis silk tie, my arm made vascular by Scottish genetics, enhanced by football, basketball, weight-lifting, wrestling, fencing, skiing, sailing, cycling, life guarding and rowing in New England lakes and on Atlantic and Caribbean seashores.

The entrance through the skin of the delicate, slim gleaming rapier, the slight withdrawing of the plunger, a blossom of a most brilliant scarlet silver flake blood bulb signally the perfect arterial alignment.

The depression of the plunger and its silver deep into the vein, the vibrating sound of joy compressed, loving embrace, and a sigh heaved in forever peace.

Even now as I write this, I feel the soft silence of the world of the needle flow overtaking me. A breath held in suspension, the sensual ambience of a moment in snowfall, gazing at the tumbling, uniquely shaped twirling wet whirly gigs mated with impossible possibilities of expansive delusions of grandeur.

If one has taken too much, this moment of joy is abruptly short, immediately transformed by the onrush of rising distinct bells ringing in the ears, an onset of momentous dizziness, world tilting in fun house imbalance.

'Zone of Bells/Room of See Saws'.

Poised before death and life, on the border where only God decides whether you live or die in a light click moment.

Willingly you give up control to your destiny, hoping to live, yet scared, even aroused by the uncertainty. I crossed many times, then standing, weaving, a beam grin on my face. I was drawn back and through athleticism and great good luck I survived when so many others did not.

It all came to an end one night after I used my Red Cross Life Guarding skill set to resurrect designer Jill Stuart from an epileptic-like seizure, mouth foaming, and eyes gone rolling white near death.

Four of us had injected 19 grams of pura. She went over 'Zone of Bells/Room of See Saws' into full unconscious collapse, her luscious buxom body spastic, a puppet whose strings were cut by a blade, her full lips bubbling bluish spit.

And when I saved her by mouth-to-mouth and violent slaps, heaving her onto her feet, forcing her to walk, her first words upon revival were, "More! I want more!" I knew then the full madness of this bit of business.

The next morning, I told myself if I was going to continue, why not simply shoot myself. It was slow suicide anyway. My skin was going; my relationship with the Israeli was in tatters, both of us sleeping with others in a bedlam of alternating jealousy and pain.

My finances were in shambles. I was living in a prized spacious apartment on Park Avenue and 63rd – sharing it with my artistic cocaine Jewish business partner, he wrapping his arm in the sacred tefillin as part of his morning religious ritual, then popping a feeble vein into ready reception of the madness needle.

I was running with Perry Ellis and the INTERVIEW Magazine crowd, doing a threesome here and there with a model and a bro, flaming out at clubs among the frolicking lascivious creatures.

But fate was at work, turning my life from one set of drives, vocations and vices to the direction the union boss of the galaxies required of me.

Without my own earthly calculation, without any personal ambition or aspiration, I was being guided and spurred to what was to become a source of fulfillment and purpose. Unknowingly, I was being propelled toward acting. Through this passage of heartbreak and social destruction, I was ushered down a disorientating slide to my coming salvation.

First, the collapse had to come, a reconstruction of my life. I walled myself away from everyone, severed the fashion agency partnership. I told my own private Hassidic dopamine dump fiend that if he ever brought coke into the apartment again, I would call the police. He raged and ludicrously proclaimed he would have me killed.

I laughed and swore never to write anything I didn't choose to write ever again. I revolted against advertising and what I then considered its superficiality, which of course it is often not.

At worst advertising is a callous, treacherous lie, at best, a swift communication perfectly conveying – wit, poignance, - a product or service with vibrancy for our lives.

To detox, I began running alone round the Central Park reservoir, allowing my athleticism and devotion to organic food and rejuvenation into my life again.

I did a number of things during this freelance period.

Standup reporting for television news carried out for WOR-TV, the 11- time Emmy award-winning Shana Alexander Show WHAT'S HAPPENING AMERICA – reporting on the additives in wine production.

Designing and revamping all packages for Publishers Clearing House sent to hundreds of millions of households every few months - direct mail rollout gigs.

I was fired from INTERVIEW by Bob Colacello again, this time permanently, for the 'hubris' of jokingly saying I was the best writer they had.

I would soon leave media and advertising to dive deep into the nobility and narcissi of the actorini.

Now you know the impulses, citizenry, codes, culture and cock lava I brought to Hollywood.

The End

Special Excerpt

Dying for Living

Sins & Confessions of a Hollywood Villain and Libertine Patriot

Vol. Two –

Showbiz

Diary of Debacle

Patrick Kilpatrick

The more work people do for me, the prettier or more handsome they become. It even causes a growth in mammary tissue & penis size.

I don't have a conscience for this stuff.

<u>Western Swerving, Golden Rape & Race Hollywood
Moments, Spielberg & Seagal ... Wives, Mistresses,
Paramours & Cross Continental Passionate Pioneers</u>

**"She wants you. She'll think of you. She'll dream of
you like some cheap gothic novel."
Byron Volpe / PARASOMNIA**

*The little cowboy in the family pictures had 'growed up,'
brimming with rehabilitated reckless spunk.*

*And just as his ancestor Ben Kilpatrick, (an unrepentant
good old boy bank/train robber who assumed leadership of
the 'Hole in the Wall Gang' when Butch and Sundance split
for Bolivia), had headed west from Alabama to Colorado
after a duel over a black woman, Patrick Kilpatrick, this
21st century 'rider', honed to literacy in the hallowed
Manhattan halls of Luce, Hearst and Hefner ... burnished
in NEW YORKIE, Kennedy Center and Williamstown
Theater Festival stage proclivities from such life forms and
luminaries as John Glover, Frank Langella, Christopher
Reeves, Richard Dreyfus, Blythe Danner, Brad Davis, Max
Caulfield, Brooke Adams, Jeff Daniels, Carol Kane and
Stockard Channing... after failing to pick up Sigourney
Weaver and Mary Elizabeth Mastrantonio, succeeding in
picking up Carly Simon and contracting crabs from
Broadway's Ann De Salvo, after off and on Broadway and
the West End of London, disparaged by Irene Worth and
held in orgasm by Shirley Knight, he arose from the dead of
cocaine and being sexual chattel, left the worlds he knew,
sortied away from the East to play with the
megalomaniacal action titans of the West.*

To stump along with those wearing the slack jawed deoxygenated pallid stroke mask ... 'Gang of Six'... Steven Seagal, JC Van Damme, Tom Sizemore, Gary Busey, Michael Madsen, Mickey Rourke (in the dark days) ... fallen actors, 'production assets' – brain matter that must be caged in a small padded cell, released only to isolated scenes, near the food truck but apart from life as we know it.

Tom Selleck, Sam Elliot, Kate Capshaw, Sean Connery, Mark Harmon, Meg Ryan, Eli Wallach, Kenny McMillian, Bruce Willis, Arnold, James Woods, Donnie Wahlberg, Vera Farmiga, George Clooney ,Vanessa Williams, Bill Paxton, Lou Ferrigno, Avery Brooks, Michael Rooker, Rampage Jackson, Stipe Miocic, Tyne Daley, Sharon Gless, Kongo, Chuck Liddell, Rosalind Cash, Chael Sonnen, Arthur Sarkissian, Ken Davidian, Chow Yun-Fat, Carl Lumbly, Maria Shriver, Till Schweiger, Kate Mulgrew, Stacey Keach, Jane Seymour, Wilford Brimley, Eric Roberts, Keith David, William Forsythe, Kevin Costner, Lee Majors, Katherine Heigl, Cheryl Ladd, Neal McDonough, Colin Farrell, Samantha Morton, Peter Stormare, Charlton Heston, Robert Stack, Sean Young, Mira Sorvino, Andy Griffith, Robert Woodward, Costas and Louis Mandylor, Summer Glau, Lena Heady, Marty Kove, Tom Cruise, Max Von Sydow Gillian Anderson, Danny de Vito, Jurgen Prochnow, Danny Trejo Robert Patrick, Ron Perlman, David Caruso, Christopher Walken, Steve Harris, Mykeletti Williamson ... Joe Tillinger, Stephen Spielberg, Chuck Russell, Antoine Fuqua, Leo Penn, Guy Hamilton, Nic Roeg, Janusz Kaminski, Walter Hill, Gilbert Adler,

James Keach, James Brolin, Lawrence Bender, Harry
Abrams, Walter Parkes, Gerald Moen, Arnold Kopelson,
Bernie Brillstein, Brad Grey, Michael Medavoy ...
Terrance McNally, Elmore Leonard, Louis L'Amour,
Phillip K. Dick, David Goyer ...

I am struck by the size of my entertainment family – names,
memories, dollops of human sweets upon the buttery toll-
house cookie sheet of a life.

QUICK & the DEAD – (Do you dream of climbing astride
a noble horse and committing cultural misappropriation?)

LAST STAND at SABER RIVER - Tom Selleck (Tom, in some countries, if you're mounted by a protagonist you're betrothed.)

DEATH WARRANT – Jean Claude Van Damme (Punishing JC's naughty bits because he can't remember his line.)

LAST MAN STANDING - Bruce Willis (Pleasure to work again with a New York trained actor after the deluge of athletes to the screen.)

First man falling in LAST MAN STANDING, blending of me and stunt double Dave Rowden. In reality I would havebeaten Bruce to the draw by so much he would have eaten a pound of .45 slugs.

REPLACEMENT KILLERS - Chow Yun-Fat (Tell me why there's a piece of paper in my cookie?)

FREE WILLY: THE RESCUE - Yes, there is a tender side to every villain.

FREE WILLY: THE RESCUE - Saved from a frigid drowning by my Orca adversary.

MINORITY REPORT & Stunt of the Year – Tom Cruise (I'll always cherish this moment with our hot asses propelling us skyward.)

Actors, directors, writers, producers, cinematographers, animators, *all the department heads and crafts people of tomorrow's new artistic horde invasion* which I hope will continually arise to thwart stagnation, boredom, studio comic book spit up, TV reboots and flawed, pitiful sequels … let's continue to do something together which simultaneously defies convention and strides on sacred world financial savvy.

*****

Pam Grier, Academy Award and Emmy nominated woman, her pink path, opulent breasts and dewy canyons previously traversed by Richard Pryor, Freddie Prinze, Kareem Abdul Jabbar.

We were both cast in a project with promise, CLASS OF 1999, location lower 48 exotic - Seattle.

I auditioned in a wheelchair, fresh calf augmentation to restore the atrophy and asymmetry of the car crash, paid by Screen Actors Guild after my impassioned plea for coverage … a chronicle of car crash, yearned for aesthetics and courageous rebuild evoking Pablo Picasso's GUERNICA, so grateful they have poetic hearts.

My athletic body fully recreated …

Just in time …

Day after being given the part – I'd lied, tossed off something like "I had minor knee repair' to explain rolling into the casting – I was encased in claustrophobic plaster by an SFX wunderkind, full body (to replicate me as a machine).

Wouldn't do to have a proportioned perfect body with chicken legs.

That procedure doesn't even exist any longer, conceived for international body builders – *Arnold allegedly.*

The calf is a tricky muscle. For some the more you work it, leaner it becomes – the market for silicon adornment expanded in that voluminous body mass STAY HUNGRY, PUMPING IRON moment.

Reveal! Three hard, inert silicon prostheses (not creamy like Pam's umber chalices), mine mirroring the actual natural muscles in the human leg, were inserted behind my calf fascia.

I was so devoured by marital frustration ... so furiously fed up with my British skyway to a retro 19th century wife, when she dropped me off at the airport, so I could wing to my CLASS OF 1999 job, as her car pulled away from the restricted area, her blond head fading to dark profile, I cursed her, vowed to heaven to have an affair the moment I arrived in the location city.

Setting down, landmark Space Needle along the sunset, playing 'ultimate cyborg' long before Schwarzenegger and his TERMINATOR, years before I played 'Terminator' on TERMINATOR: THE SARAH CONNOR CHRONICLES (glowing Summer Glau and ultra-Lena Headey) that's exactly what I did - dive headlong into double dip dark Dairy Queen.

Laying eyes on Grier, a brief dinner with others, a confession of marital dissatisfaction, I was buried in her wild mouth and dark mass of hair.

Gallantless journalista...

It was everything you weren't, you imperious, entitled, oppressive wife ... Oh sweet baby Jesus on a stick, life is too short!

Pam, anyone's top three female action icons, first African American woman to headline an action flick ... lovely molten actor, eternal sex symbol, world's 1st female action Queen to Quentin Tarantino.

She was emotional and lacking in confidence. Fresh from cancer terror and prescribed hysterectomy, tragically (if one believes in tragedy) barren, saddled with momentary tremulous esteem, doubting her femininity.

'Little Black Pambo' (my bedroom nickname for her) couldn't have been more wrong - she's Cleopatra.

Rain takes me to a place of cleansed air and ion filled contentment and memory, Pam was physical, verbal, sound and touch flashing fresh on the lagoon of lust and love, bright bolts of blue lightening and seasonal thunder.

Surrounded by men early, she curses easily. We loved playing with John P. Ryan (RUNAWAY TRAIN, CARNAL KNOWLEDGE), Malcolm McDowell and Stacey Keach, one-time 'American Olivier'.

McDowell ... subdued, watch him and mutter, "He's phoning it in! (*Historically similar reports when Gary Cooper worked.*) Then you observe the film result, works.

When my wife visited set, I'd leave our hotel room and go down the hall to Pam, replacing the wife deliciously, scampering about in succulent farce.

I wrote a thousand poems to Pam, conch silk phrases of adoration.

One day in a misplaced rage of hurt and jealousy she would tell me she burned each and every one and the computer where they were stored.

I willfully stuck two and a half inches of my middle finger up the ass bud of another actor.

The probe was made more intrusive by the thick khaki cloth of his pants, so the 'wound channel' had girth, a thickened cigar like bulk. Cavitation - the size of the shockwave and disruption - to his buttocks and central nervous system was immediately intense. Anyone who knows weapons and bullet testing on ballistic gel will understand graphically and visually.

I was on an 'unorthodox' independent road trip film directed by Christopher Coppola, Nic Cage's brother, Francis Ford's nephew - PALMERS PICKUP - Bobby Carradine, Rosanna Arquette, Soupy Sales, Alice Ghostly, Talia Shire as the Devil.

Cast and crew literally climbed into a yellow school bus in the Burger King parking lot off Wilshire and away we went, fitfully halting at eclectic Americana stops for one take filming discipline.

You had to be fast, perfect, kill it right out of the box, especially in areas above the snow line. Otherwise company tracks in the pure driven white stuff would spoil the shot, crush the suspension of disbelief.

I lived for 28 days on Ambien and coffee, with a massage at every stop, late into the night, not easy to procure in the dimly lit, decaying strip malls and rural landscape of coast to coast America.

The film premise - I played a homosexual, homicidal Navy SEAL, fresh from prison. At script's opening, I arrive back at prison gate with my pet Chihuahua Judy, picking up my male lover in a rudely orange Dodge Charger ragtop. The two of us catapult forward on a commission from the Devil, to pursue a moving van, driven by Bobby Carradine, carrying a 'Doomsday' device of indeterminate nature.

In one demented memorable scene, I torture and drown Alice Ghostly (BEWITCHED) in a festive bowl of eggnog.

We had auditioned the part of my lover extensively, Peter Tork of the Monkees among the failed aspirants. Finally, a man came in that was just right, playing off me like a squat, deranged, pasty matador. You could feel the exhilaration of the find.

Our bus slips away eastward, my head out the skylight roof windows to escape the crew chain-smoking, watching stars emerging from the stink-hole pollution, sucking oxygen on the climb to the mountains.

My 'actor' lover starts banging grass and hitting pills as soon as we exited inland. It's clear to me he is that most despicable of creatures, the 'audition magician', with no real interest in the craft beyond, no inner character lashing him to excellence. In a word, he was scum.

When a production is on a tight schedule, the pros get going.

The production ritual at each stop became by necessity ... do the master shot – the entire scene - then my close up, wham got it, one take, then shift camera, his close up, drugged, dead, abysmal, lackluster.

We found ourselves in a scene in the desert – the picture car convertible top down, parked on a lonely road, popping magic hour light, eternal luminescence of strip mall Western cobalt sky and approaching stars.

My cinematic character is longing for sex and love, hungering for my lover, incessantly groping and kissing him, even as he squirms in filmic and real time pill induced lethargy.

Bang one take for my closeup – then nothing from the other idiot's side. Complete facial and body banality …

The small camera and sound crew were frustrated, sighing in the still air, just desperately wanting the shot so we could scurry to our one-night hotel home.

I stuck my thick ring finger full force into my acting partner's ass. Left it there, lingering, twirling a bit, gouging deeper. He screamed, wrenched through and above the peeled back roof, bleating in insult and agony. As if the bulbous lollipop were attempting to escape the stick.

Brilliant, said the crew! Got it! Exquisite! Yes, sir! Pack it up, going home!

As we rode to the hotel, my movie lover was stunned, darkly brooding. Pressed hard against the window glass of the transpo van interior, features shrouded in something like retardation – a roofied Charles Loughton, pale and exhausted by a rigorous day as Quasimodo – a *dinner break*

in the local squalid men's room for ass impaling with
rigorous mouth fucking, then home to Elsa - he was alone
in sullen trauma, all of us laughing, content, genius in the
can, mission well done, traversing cactus and sage dusk.

The next day he arrived at the set waving a highly theatrical
machete, cursing me - not with me there of course - but to
Christopher.

"I'M GOING TO FUCKING SUE THIS FUCKING
MOVIE AND THAT FUCKER!" he screamed in my
absence.

He disappeared when I arrived.

I was tickled pink as Coppola conveyed the diatribe. This is
exactly what this tiny, embryonic flick needs! Free
publicity on a heroic level!

I could see the case unfold on national television and
tabloids. Being sued for male-on-male sexual (rape)
harassment, egregious, liscentious assault, during a broad
daylight homosexual ravaging for celluloid! I could hear
the discourse, the judicial jockeying, the nature of creation
and reality! Imagination and technique! Sordid
controversy, set-side rectal brutality! (Harvey Weinstein's
looming visage at Ago - doughy, pockmarked, inquiring
bloat - aglow with his thoughts of prerelease genius for
frothed-up controversial hype). Rejoicing among the circus
freaks!

There was after all no controversy with Jewish leaders over
LIFE IS BEAUTIFUL (Best Picture) and its purported
trivialization of the Holocaust, no PASSION OF CHRIST

Mel Gibson dust up with the Jewish community over millennia complicity for the Messiah's torturous death. All of it made up, skillful media confetti to make Moe and Flo scramble to Arclight or Metroplex.

This is exactly right, legal alarm and filth! It will make Jean Claude's COURT TV slash and stab of truth and extras, his plunging into eyes with rubber knives and crushing of noses, his base lies, subterfuge and perjury - all of that nothing compared with anal revilement in the sacred cause of art!

The director wanted nothing of it.

"No!" said Chris. You can't call him Chris by the way - in his youth bullies abused him "Chris Piss, Chris Piss!"

Pearls of PR lost, squandered opportunity. I'm simply the Executive Officer, no, lowly swabbie sailor, alright a jovial Lieutenant. Helm as you will, Christopher.

I've always considered the dual tactical strokes of simultaneous flanking embrace kissed by full frontal confrontation the perfect answer to asinine behavior.

The filming continued, loser lover boy kept his distance. The movie story unfolded. Boiling with frustration, my resisting lover kills my beloved doggie, Chihuahua Judy.

I then strangle him, crying out in loss and righteous revenge. *Chris wrote the thing, for Christ sake.*

Still loving him – necrothespianiac mourning, I take his body, Jeffrey Dahmer-like, and delicately tie his barely clothed corn beef and hash form to the banana seat of the stolen chopped motorcycle that had replaced the now decimated, discarded Charger.

I was heavily made up by then. My character had toppled into electrocution and blistering scarring amidst a burning holiday fir tree. Wearing a sheer peach negligee and shower cap, faux flames had consumed my face and hands. I resembled a creature adorned with raw scarlet beef, white eyes and red pupils peering from shriveled epidermal crisp.

Christopher and I huddled daily to costume the corpse of my lover, each day a new insult to the addled homophobe.

His body was not good, his breasts saggy, belly furred and distended with flab ... a pink tutu and western boots one night, a polypropylene tube top and mini skirt the next ... night after night, garbing my fucked up darling with demented Barbie wardrobe in tandem with Manhole Fantasy or Mud Pie Versace, gauche and gaudy, through Texas, Mississippi, Georgia, down to Florida ... and it was frigid on those long night motorcycle shoots, wind racing over his shivering flesh folds.

We tortured him, and he deserved every second, for there is nothing viler than an actor who fails to deliver the goods, nothing so foul, so deserving of scorn and indignity.

A thousand fingers up the ass of actors who fail to bring it.

*****

In a small town in Pennsylvania I directed a sequence about terrorist killers who seize a historic paddle wheeler transformed to a 21st century tourist ship plying the waters of Lake Erie from Canada to America.

Wishing 'authenticity' and since rape often occurs in these takeover situations, I had the bright idea of asking volunteers from the local crowd to serve as sexual assault victims. Embarrassed, tentative, feeling soiled I called for takers among the female excursionists.

The trip was weird to begin, a wedding was taking place on the boat that day and the couple had agreed to our filming while they celebrated. Who in their right mind wants explosions, smoke bombs, an *actual* S. W. A. T team (Erie, PA) and blank loaded automatic weapons spitting flame and ear rupturing simulated death on the occasion of their nuptials? Small town America(!) of course.

They rushed me, women volunteers of all types, teachers, a psychologist, housewives, even the bride, clamored gleefully forward to be digitally filmed rape victims. To lie down on the deck, have their pants, skirts, wedding gown hiked, tops and under garments shoved aside judiciously and then be mounted and dry ground by strange large men as other strangers skittered about lighting and filming. What I would consider demeaning, they yearned for, achieved completion through.

I realized the overpowering need for fantasy in our lives. A man of Hollywood like myself, who play acts for a living, who dresses up and becomes a corrupt CIA operative, a damaged football star, a demonic obsessed priest, a morally challenged whaler or stressed out cowboy … I barely fully conceive of the thirst of the populace for play acting expression.

Out of their boredom with work and stultifying relationships comes Halloween's growth market costume billions, STAR TREK convention proliferation, DUNGEONS AND DRAGONS, CALL TO DUTY: BLACK OPS, TRANSFORMERS outer limit gross revenues … renaissance fairs to reality shows, civilities decay to mass active shooters living in imagined filmic moments as they gun down the innocent.

The primal need to delude and dream/nightmare away desperation is always there.

Having in many instances lost the ability to live life with creativity, to seek challenge in survival and triumph amidst far reaches of earth and space, to gather insight and learning by reading and art, much of our species has numbed its sensitivities to holocaust and mass savagery. Now we adorn our psyches with low aspiration, colorless media inaccuracies - all without having the vocabulary to describe the sensations.

One highly memorable moment: We were filming a beautiful local girl, not an actress, in close-up. I had devised a potentially devastating but poignant moment as the terrorist points his weapon at her face at the moment of her execution.

She looks simply into the camera an utters, "I have two children." Then she is killed.

I couldn't get the girl, lovely as she was, to possess in her eyes the necessary pathos and imploring. I reached across the lens and gently swiped my fingers across her chin, hoping to get the startled light of surprise in her expression.

Sweet teenage Jesus, she collapsed! Weeping and trembling in terror! In a fraction of an instant, knowing well this could destroy the entire production, *not to mention my being hailed as 'an assaulter of actors'*, I enveloped her in my arms, turned swiftly with her sobbing and pinwheeled off the set, repeating over and over, "I love you, I love you, I love you, it's alright!!! You're beautiful!" into her aromatic hair and neck.

As she descended from this absolute panic, me cooing and soothing, I asked what was this all about.

"My boyfriend beat me up last week," she whimpered.

Holy Christ directing can be touchy!

One last slap: On MARTIAL LAW, the number one show of the year in 1998, I was the villain, Arsenio Hall the detective hero along with Sammo Kam-Bo Hung, an immensely popular martial arts figure worldwide. The scene called for me to interrogate Arsenio's character. As cameras rolled he grew glib and snarky under my Q & A. So I reached across and slapped him hard. The set sucked in a collective gasp.

The scene played out perfectly. Never surrender your character's goals.

In the interest of full disclosure, I should mention that Arsenio and I had shared biblical congress with the same truly pretty, but highly neurotic gang anal rape victim woman. I swear that had no impact on my impulse to slap.

One last fight with WWE's 'Stone Cold' Austin: I was interrogating him as well, he resisted, actually began to fight with me. Not a good idea to escalate against the script. So, I ended up on top of him on the floor. My character had no other choice. The director loved it, laughed as he netted in camera the continuing pageant of actors/athletes/humans being pups of ego.

*****

Two vignettes from the current 'sexual harassment' #metoo buffet: Bai Ling (or Ling Bai – if one wishes to embrace the Chinese structure for her name. I don't wish to embrace anything to do with China until they stop being communist freedom stranglers and vast intellectual property thieves which isn't coming anytime soon since a tsunami of global companies don't give a damn what the politics or justice component of a nation are – US included) … Bai Ling, delicate and individualistically offbeat in the most beautiful way *and from the moon as she professes* and I had lunch on Larchmont Boulevard to talk about being in a film I was contemplating.

The lunch was my treat of course, I hold holy the respect and adoration of the male/female producer/actor pattern. Men and producers pay. *Ms. Ling is allegedly all about the money and herself. Producing an event years ago my sponsors large and small refused to contribute if I invited her. It seems she was taking sponsor swag and eBaying it immediately. Sponsors provide celebrities with items to have the celeb visibly use the items, curry press coverage of the product and extend their marketing to influencers, not offer actors side cash in the flea market of life. Perhaps she was critically short of moola. Eye candy alone only brings in so much.*

After the luncheon we strolled the small street, passing kiosks and flung open stores. We came to a small boutique offering perfect dresses, shifts, skirts – each a colorful, finely crafted expression.

I said, "Why don't you pick a dress? It would be my honor to get it for you."

She stepped into the center of the store, attentive salesgirls hovering, dropped slipped the dress she was wearing, stood in profile with nothing on but heels. She then effortlessly tried on dresses one after another until she selected one, each change punctuated by full nudity, each moment filled with the display of her exquisite body.

The effect for me – after a moment of shock and feeling uncomfortable for her - was akin to gazing at an early rotoscope of girl loveliness – part child porn – she is quite small, tiny moon breasts and finely boned – yet all glowing woman, with a bit of enigmatic glamour.

Oh for sweet Jesus sake! Hold the fucking venetian blind and I'll fuck it.

Thoughts and impulses flashed through me. She was intentionally shocking me, seducing me as a man and producer. She was exerting her control over the space, the street and her body.

It also occurred that she was perhaps like me, groomed from fast wardrobe fittings and changes through 160 films and TV shows. I own one pair of underwear solely for wardrobe fittings which I invariably forget and in so doing the fitting at some point becomes a bare as a jaybird prance. I regularly change in parking lots for meetings, quickly and at least for a moment completely nude.

I'm sure if the opposite were true, had I dropped my trousers in Neanderthal display for street and store patrons, LAPD S.W.A.T. would have been summoned, rubber bullets discharged at my genitalia, a civil suit by outraged Hancock Park residents initiated replete with psychological/lost earning cost estimates, a press conference/rally with PTSD victims hawked by Gloria Allred and Lisa Bloom, penning up shell shocked 'member wounded' into a heroic gaggle of self-congratulatory weeping, reports of nightmares and thwarted 'good' relations with current boyfriends and husbands – a Netflix Original Documentary.

*****

Actors always protest "sex scenes are so awkward". Home front propaganda I'm sure, something to say to keep real boyfriends, wives, husbands, girlfriends off the pungent scent of sets on fire. "It wasn't fun, uncomfortable, the crew is milling around, it's hot and chafing!" I suspect they're merely keeping it in their pants verbally for the public and the life partners.

Charlize Theron being interviewed on the torrid lesbian sex for ATOMIC BLOND (best fight scenes ever) - "We're both dancers," she licked out, which truthfully implies rampant aerial acrobatics, a great deal of orgasmic fluidity, hitting marks with pinpoint acceleration.

Ever curious, I asked the love of my life one time, after she mentioned having sex with a male bi-sexual ballet partner in her twenties, how it was.

My lady of four years, as rambunctious, smart and funny as they come and having journeyed through Vegas, Paris, and New York as a global showgirl flung her mane backward and with a combination of haughty disdain and near insult cried out ... "WE WERE DANCERS!!!!!" Endless ecstasies, gyro scoping infusion - Good God! – *let not even the supremely secure inquire.*

I've had a great deal of fun and enjoyment in all my sex scenes - violent assault or romantic coupling. It wasn't awkward at all, but revelatory.

*****

Angie Everhart - a neophyte 'actress,' initially infamous as the lover/fiancé of action star Sylvester Stallone, was hired on this particular film for $80,000 with a 'nudity' proviso, a bare tits component of cable movies after 10PM. The mandatory topless display in that environment is as basic and required as low budgets, automatic weapons and lame-to-the-spoon drug use plotting.

No problem on my end, no ego, that's cool. She dripped Playboy model notoriety and gossipy potential. That was the very raison d'etre for her being there and I am nothing if not a student of filmic scandal well played for sales potential.

She was getting four times my pay - objectively possessing maybe twenty-five per cent of the acting chops held by me or anyone else on the set. The core basis of her contract was the obligatory topless baring which is a structural underpinning of almost everything after 10PM on HBO, endemic soft core on cable.

The devolved audience presumably would peak at the prospect of peeking the translucent, luminescent mammary, dusted with Celtic gold freckles, a justifiable and covetable marquee attribute.

Day one - she began to give every person (except me) on the set a hard time.

The most reprehensible brats and cowards rarely give me grief. It might have to do with the fact they take one gaze at me and falsely believe I will torture them if they do, simple outward scariness.

I have the look of a psychopathic assassin but in reality, I am usually merely prowling for a massage, a hot almond milk 16 oz. flat white alongside carob banana coconut gluten-free pancakes and an organic strawberry carrot juice with a side of pussy.

The red-haired actress was abusive, refusing to come out of the trailer, disrespecting the director (Robert Radler), camera personnel, craft service, PA's ... one and all were touched under her litany of rude misbehavior.

The problem, of course, stemmed from her 'seller's remorse' to do the breasts shots which were a pillar of the rough near rape romp scheduled with my character.

I was slightly amused, with little sympathy. You get paid for something, you do the job - particularly when one considers Ms. Everhart had revealed body and limb in other films, starting with ANOTHER 9 ½ WEEKS (with maestro of manners at the time Mickey Rourke). Her reticence was petulant and misplaced.

The filming took place in the Deep South at a classical, prestigious boys' prep military academy. In the quadrangle stood a small memorial to slain graduates, young boy/men who ascended from the school and laid down their lives for us... males who had consumed and alchemized the ideals of America, went on to be disemboweled by artillery fire, slaughtered, weeping, tragically terrified and sacrificially noble, each a symbol for our finest instincts and basest loss. Their names, whispers and smiles resonated throughout the bricked architecture, their never-realized lovemaking and children never born, each one's years of life swept away by war.

I was playing a white Aryan Army Airborne Ranger, the school commandant honing supremacist cog boys at the debased prep academy.

Rough sex, pedophilic manipulation, soiling of the GRAND TRADITIONS of National Service and Our Warriors, vicarious quasi pornography with conjugal punch outs of movie action heroes - this c-film follow-up had all the exploitation pillars. Treat Williams, Bill Nunn, Simon Rhee, Tim Abel and I cavorting with curvaceous titian domed Angie. Whoopee doo!!!

*****

Across town was the Martin Luther King Museum, a four-block national federal park, fully illuminative in its interweaved signposts to the man's origins - son of a preacher, grandson to a preacher, spawn from learned men of articulation, Baptist African American rhyme and oratory.

One day I went to the MLK site with a distinct mission in mind.

Reared in color-blind Connecticut, clasped in honor bound revolutionary Virginia, I had rarely even considered racism or gender/identity even as a concept.

I grew up with black members in small 'secret' brotherhood fraternities in both New England and Richmond.

Now as I walked slowly through the museum halls I was bathed in a legacy of genocidal lynching, racial rape

286

reprisal, kids murdered for winking at white women - the foulest expressions of Caucasian cruelty.

I felt guilty, even deeply ashamed for being white by the time I was minutes into the exhibit.

I was trailed closely through the exhibit by a class of high school blacks, grinning, watching, certainly all being lashed into such distress, such primordial rage; surely, I would become target of 'colored' fury!

Swiftly exiting, employing the Robert De Niro (a *point man artist now skittered away into anti-Trump erratic displays)* ability to move sideways on a street, invisibly, converting self to two muted camo dimensions, eschewing polychromatic 3-D, making my beeline to the rental car.

The heart-of-anger mob followed, quickening their pace, teeth bared, gleefully tasting the stalk, *knowing* not only was I white, fact alone enough to elicit a castration, sensing too, yes, I come from slave holding rebel seed, *not just THIS*, but I was there exercising a sick, artistically-impure impulse.

I was here at the King shrine to gather his speeches and writings, then paraphrase and transform Reverend King's baptismal epic prose and vocal mastery into psalms of hate and reactionary rationalization for the shit-ass movie and my character's mongrel new age KKK spew... "I had a nightmare, I have seen the filth of multiculturalism!"

The dark mob accelerated into a gallop, now adding baying, insane laughter to stoke their revenge, jet fuel to reptilian blood lust hate.

I choked on terror, fumbled badly for the keys. Too late! Their oversize teeth loomed enlarged, each bellowing, keening with cannibal exaltation!

All I could do was go down, ball up like a centipede, protect head and testicles, hope the sack eggs and face survive the onslaught, pray no blades or spiked war clubs come out.

"He's in the movies! He's on TV!!!! MOVIES!!!"

The love washed over me with their bodies, their smiles, sculpted dark hands stroked my clothing on my back, arms, caressing my skull and face ... propulsive exhalations of survival and gratitude fell from me on the parking lot of the MLK Fed Park. I was alive and being joyfully massaged by 'The Other'.

****

I returned to the movie and Angie Everhart, scrolls, transcripts and posters of the great orator's speeches and writings in hand.

Preparing for the rough love scene with the 'actress' I consumed an entire Viagra. I am a large man but hyper-sensitive to stimulants, even coffee is wild meth shot into my veins.

I had a design in mind.

Viagra, Cialis, Levitra - nuances, psychological and physiological, a samba festival of sexual versatility and vulnerabilities - perhaps for another seminar … this was simple on set juvenility with a justice twinge.

I careened into the scene, becoming cast and crew's sword, Round Table "Might for Right" penile Excalibur, unsheathed in walk-down-a-jungle Errol Flynn foolery.

She had dappled mammary, prominent ruby rosettes. Her brown and white eyes were wild with annoyance and trepidation. The crew was burbling with suppressed knowing.

My job, clearly dictated by the script, was to grasp the ungrateful, impolite, abrasive actress's hips, as she rode me … rake borderline painful fingers over her impressionable flesh, cup and maul the infamous tits, tracing red white bloodless contrails, *no lasting bruising.*

Lips delicately biting, hands tangling her hair, reining Ms. Everhart into my mouth, laughing/experiencing the performance art of my hopped up giant white Grand Prize gourd flailing the flimsy flesh colored G-strings issued us.

The camera team was having trouble pulling focus for the bobbing, unavoidable objet.

Angie writhed, not in passion, but rather in extreme discomfiture, a lake of embarrassment surrounded by a director crew and myself convulsed in near spitting giggles. We held check, even as my prick, rigid and angling upward, kneaded and bumped her sex and belly. It had to be pushed aside by my hand so as not to continually enter camera frame.

She might have captured us all had she found humor and enlisted her wit. *But no.*

The sequence was achieved.

One is not on the set to be difficult, to betray contacts or contracts, not there to be unkind, but to emanate the spirit of individual and polite offering, to script, director, audience, to yourself by virtue of craft.

One is there to create with courage, intelligence and dynamic choices; always carrying a bit of humility with the waking moment … there to SERVE and to uplift. To lead each other to our finer being, whether through depraved comedy or universal drama, inspiring stage combat, scathing political and social indictment or untamed emotional catharsis.

Whenever I see Angie about town, at this event and that, she smiles at me knowingly. A hyper large cock - even when pill induced, conjured in mischief - somehow carries with it an enduring female empathy.

I pulled off the morphing of Martin Luther King's speech for the movie in spirited fashion. I ranted and raved in recognizable paraphrasing of his eternal words, transformed the Gandhi precepts into bile of violence, mutilating his poetry in the service of cinema villainy.

The remarkable thing - it was white, politically correct studio executives who became nervous with the choices, blacks chuckled and reveled in it the world over. "You're the best racist supremacist ever!" I've been told lovingly to this day.

I am grateful to black audiences. Rabid action fans with some sort of antagonist radar; they were the first cultural group to actually appreciate what I was doing as an actor, followed next by Asian and Hispanic audiences.

It has been a remarkable source of surprise and delight to move about the globe and instantly be recognized by people of color. I have tried to understand this affection. Perhaps many minorities feel an affinity for those who revolt against the 'Man' as movie villains do; a way to cast aside tiny daily oppressions and insults. It's a message to me to grasp for my ascendant angels.

*****

My character attempted to rape Daphne Zuniga's characterin the TV movie STONE PILLOW, Lucille Ball's last job before her death. It was a great honor to work with the legend, but raping actresses on-camera is truly a thankless task. Before I terrorized Daphne (MELROSE PLACE) on camera I gently offered, "This isn't me, it's my character".

It didn't help.

They can be interested in you beforehand, perhaps want to flirt with you, even date you, but once you mentally and/or physically maul them in the scene, the relationship goes south.

291

In a profession founded on extraordinary vision, we pack less of it than perhaps we should.

After the scene, Daphne looked at me differently and treated me like filth.

I'm not talking about my character actually hurting someone, of course. Nor the laying on of hands in any action of the scene - a breakdown in craft, an abomination avoided at all cost.

Doing a vile cinematic act with passion and emotional conviction is your job, not your personhood. It's acting darlings and friends.

I auditioned for a Broadway production of STREETCAR NAMED DESIRE and here came the Williamstown Theater hierarchy once more. The production was directed by Nikos Psacharopoulos to star Blythe Danner. It was a return of sorts to my first contact with these renown creators at the Williamstown Theater Festival.

My initial audition in Los Angeles for Nikos was with Cheryl Ladd, a wonderful if 2-dimensional TV persona, an original CHARLIE'S ANGELS alumnus. Cheryl, reading the Blanche Dubois role against my Stanley, was wholly unprepared for the intensity and near homicidal inferno of the scene.

I consumed her, which is exactly what Stanley does to Blanche, the tempo Marlon Brando carried out against Vivien Leigh in the original film. Vivien was somewhat prepared to counter and thrive, Cheryl was not. It worked for me, not for Cheryl. She was stunned and shattered while I was flown to New York to audition with Blythe.

I respect Blythe Danner; I felt considerate of her, deferential - wrong impulse for an actor in a scene, particularly that piece. I pulled back to the detriment of the audition. I learned to never pull back … but to plunge, maneuver, storm forward ruthlessly with my character's goals - that is so important to the journey and the text. Instead of being on Broadway I received an extremely complimentary letter from Nikos, saying I was superb but that his decision - which Stanley to cast - was made based on several factors among several superb candidates.

They chose Aidan Quinn - more famous at the time in New York Circles. Wrong choice, Aidan is a fine actor. I'm sure the choice completed some bent antenna marketing box office quest they had in their head.

The production closed in two weeks.

Aidan Quinn is no Stanley, no ravager, no rapist, *no animal,* and Stanley is of course an animal, loving to Stella (within maximum parameters of a 'good relationship' and over the border in the assault of Blanche). Therein lies his sexual power and consuming beauty. He gets the animalistic job done - just as Brando was all those things - a deliverer of the goods for good or evil - a rapist lover in thug sensuous lashed package. There are many, of both sexes, who will indeed say #metoo, please, please please when the Kraken arrives in his proper beauty/ theatrical/cinematic and living setting.

It is not just a male thing. Ellen Barkin is an animal in her work. Call her a Venus flytrap - a carnivorous honeypot consuming her artistic companions in sweet but corrosive nectar. You're going to enjoy the act even as you disintegrate, melt away screaming. Is such a performer or partner going to be sated by anything less than an equal or better yet more powerful *and intricately delicate* beast.?

For it is the fury and the tenderness, the paradox combination - the opposites colliding and melding that makes for great lovemaking, great art, great cinema, dance, great acting or music.

When I was an advertising writer at TIME, INC. we often chose a picture that had one compelling effect on the viewer, then matched it with a headline of complete opposite meaning. An example - a picture of a mud-splattered football player, sprawling exhausted, defeated, weeping on the locker room floor. Match that with a headline - *The Great American Male* - and then write your way out of the paradox in the ad copy.

Great actors often go in the opposite direction of the writing - or as we have called it - *the writer shit*. If the writer says 'he weeps', instead I laugh, it says he softly burps, we loudly belch, whatever, the living moment of creation is divorced from *the writer shit*.

Tender and tough, rough yet gentle. Strangling yet deeply kissing.

*****

To play villains, to some extent one can't win for losing.

If I play a serial killer skillfully with escalating abandon and intelligence, even hardcore casting professionals and directors with long credits may view me with suspicion. It's flattering really. They have bought into my artifice reality.

To their flawed reasoning, I must somewhere in my makeup actually be a killer, a narcissist, or psychopath.

I can hear you snickering! Shut up!

They assume I must be, in real life, actually difficult or uncontrolled. In my case that may be accurate occasionally, normally not and never on set.

Naomi Watts was intrigued by me as we began to play together on a TV pilot called SLEEPWALKERS, directed by gothic helmsman Bill Malone (FEAR.COM, HOUSE ON HAUNTED HILL, PARASOMNIA). I could tell she fancied me. This isn't my grandiose egoism. We all can generally tell when another human is attracted to us or tweaked intrigued at the least. A multitude of men (and women) of power or need clearly possess a warped prism through which each view and mutate attraction, seduction, courtship, gender play and arousal. It's amusing really – accomplished 'men' with money dedicated to non-commitment and 'playerdom' locked in karmic battle with 'desirable' women scrambling for sanctuary from professional toil and economic independence.

My role called for me to kidnap Naomi's character, hurl abuse and terror upon her character for three days. I went to

Naomi before we shot and quietly chatted with her. "I have to come at you. It's my character. It's not me. Please remember that." I liked her too, considered going out with her myself. She was so talented and exceptional. *(A bit of a pale, fragile appearing sprite which wasn't my un-evolved Neanderthal sensibility type at the time, then I liked to buckle on rappelling gear and ascend mountains. I was also coming from a divorce with a British woman, a journey akin to fighting the Viet Cong, low intensity warfare of particularly brutal body count attrition. So, the Commonwealth chick thing had gone a little stale for me - eventually I would get over it and stop blaming all the Queen's females for one rampant example.)*

After the shoot, Naomi was so traumatized she would not speak to me for three years, and even then, with deep melancholic suspicion.

Ah well, it's a price to pay but worth the cost. What counts, what is of eternal value to your life and an audience is what's on the stage or screen.

The funny thing is, if you watch Naomi in KING KONG, the role that catapulted her to stardom, Watts is doing exactly the same acting with the big ape as she did with me. I guarantee you casting people and Peter Jackson, the director of KING KONG, saw her acting reel with me raging about her and her blonde nymph manipulating and mentally seducing/charming my big simian beastie. I wonder if she dated the monkey after the shoot. I hope she did well by marrying and having children with the accomplished Liev Schreiber.

Naomi's single again, perhaps redemption and sexual nirvana ahead for this unrepentant romantic and Lord Shiva bad guy.

In Hollywood - "Oh you're a newlywed! That means I can't date you for at least a year!"

I'm in a relationship now of boundless love and commitment, one that encircles and breathes life to my soul, wouldn't change a thing or seek another. Just saying lol.

Now for you Mia ... love of my life. This will become a love story of existence changing dimension.

In wee hours as I lie on the suede designer couch, flickering images of UFC knockouts on the widescreen, fondling, empowering my cock, suddenly I must have you Mia... rising quickly, entering the bedroom my nimble fingers find the jar of organic coconut oil, I watch you sleeping for a moment, stroking to hot viscosity, adjusting to the blue dark, considering exact points of clutching velvet covers to fling them open exposing you, a strong clutch at your ankle, a break dance spin of your nude dancer legs on Boylan Branch cotton, you utter moans of equal part startling incomprehensibility and impending pleasure ... I thrust into you as you cling upward ... good to be bad and tangential in thought ...

It is good to be a Libertine Patriot.

Disgusted by dilettantes in my youth, laughingly describing myself as 'cursed with Liberal Arts learning' - traversing worlds, heading West to 'work', just as the founding fathers and the horde wave they assembled clawed a continent into submission.

I have come to absolute dilettantism, an actor writer director teacher speaker patriot with Movie Black Belt.

Be not afraid of the 'Libertine Patriot' ... it is a fine tradition bathed in the bewitching spirit of the all souls of America. Jefferson and Franklin - Libertine Patriots,

saturated as much in the salons of Paris and the Worldly
Age of Enlightenment as in fiery revolution. Bon vivant
seductive animal scholar poets of freedom.

Consider their inhalation of life essential to their spirit as
architects of their age?

End Special Excerpt

Represented for Publishing, Film, TV and Stage by

Uncommon Dialogue Films, Inc.

570 N. Rossmore Ave.

Suite 203

Los Angeles, Ca. 90004

323 252 8702

Kilpatrick203@gmail.com

One of the finest screen/television actors of all time,
playing against a spectrum of Hollywood's leading action
heroes, Patrick Kilpatrick's career has spanned more than
170 films and television shows as lead actor, producer,
screen writer, director and global entertainment teacher –
Spielberg's MINORITY REPORT with Tom Cruise to
James Cameron's DARK ANGEL - the largest production
in Public Broadcasting history, off and on Broadway, West
End of London to Los Angeles Theater Center with

Academy Award winning British director Tony Richardson in Shakespeare's ANTHONY & CLEOPATRA.

Literate & genteel, savage on screen.

Murderous bi-polar assaults by an adulterous mother, vivid privileged education amidst Thoreau splendor & American Revolution patriotism, athletics mimicking his Underwater Demolition Team decorated father, bi-racial affairs & indiscriminate promiscuity, multinational marriages, incendiary politics, illiberal liberals & retrograde Republicans, South American correspondent with rampant cocaine injection, asthma, near fatal paralytic car accident & flaming hallucinatory motorcycle crashes, a global vison for America in the 21st century.

Kilpatrick's action film villain appearances embrace a multitude of genres and an international Who's Who of directors, writers, production talent, leading men and women of the last quarter century. The Replacement Killers (director Antoine Fuqua) against Yun-Fat Chow, Arnold Schwarzenegger and James Caan in Eraser (Chuck Russell), Last Man Standing (Walter Hill), opposite Bruce Willis, Under Siege 2: Dark Territory (Geoff Murphy), opposite Steven Segal, The Presidio (Peter Hyams), opposite Sean Connery and Mark Harmon, 3 award-winning westerns opposite Tom Selleck, Last Stand at Saber River (Elmore Leonard) and Crossfire Trail, with Sam Elliot and Kate Capshaw, HBO's Premiere Films adaptation of Louis L'Amour's The Quick and the Dead, and action mainstay Death Warrant (1990) opposite Jean-Claude Van Damme, as 'The Sandman', and freezing wet battle with the largest mammal on earth in Free Willy 3: The Rescue (1997).

Kilpatrick has ripped through over 75 hit TV shows - 24, DR. QUINN MEDICINE WOMAN, NIP/TUCK, TERMINATOR: SARAH CONNER CHRONICLES, CHUCK, BURN NOTICE, all CSI & NCIS franchises, James Wood's SHARK, BOOMTOWN, CRIMINAL MINDS and COLD CASE - a record of unparalleled audition/performance prowess.

Movie Black Belt

Jiu Jitsu, boxing, wrestling humpback dwarfs, sniper, pistol & shotgun, Close Quarter Battle, LAPD and SEAL TEAM /MARINE RECON training, precision driving, fencing, setting himself on fire, plunging thru glass two pistols blazing

Renaissance Beast

Carnality in the Roy Rogers Museum

Flee, Hide your Wives

Studio Theft, Agency Lies, Hollywood Peers of Cataclysmic Indulgence & Organic Brain Damage.

Scoundrel Infidel Son of Rebellion Unafraid to Speak the Truth

Patrick Kilpatrick's DYING FOR LIVING Sins and Confessions of a Hollywood Villain and Libertine Patriot - the one book every Hollywood aficionado must consume.

301